WHEN THE SEATBELT SIGN GOES OFF

Nichole L. Davis

CONTENTS

ACT III

INTRODUCTION:
WELCOME ABOARD

Whoever said that life is all about the journey, and not the destination, never worked a five-hour flight with three screaming babies, twelve needy first-class passengers, and two annoying coworkers.

Otherwise they would know: it's all about the destination.

It's about getting there and getting everyone on and off the plane as quickly as possible. It's the sigh of relief when you hear the landing gears descend after three days of nonstop flying from city to city.

It's the polite, angelic chime when the seatbelt sign goes off at the gate, letting everyone know that it's time to grab their things and go.

Because, once at the destination, the way-too-long journey is finally over and life – my *real* life – off the plane begins.

At least that's how I look at it.

On the plane, I'm simply the flight attendant. The one with the drinks, snacks, and friendly yet firm demeanor (well, most of the time).

But off the plane, away from the airport and out of uniform, I'm Nichole, a single thirty going-on-forty-something Black woman. I'm a daughter, sister, auntie, and red wine drinker trying to live my life to the fullest.

So, of course, I like to travel in search of new adventures and experiences. If you're a Facebook friend or Instagram follower, you'll find pictures of me sipping wine in Venice, petting elephants in Thailand, and riding camels in Morocco. From the outside looking in, I'm a wild and free gypsy spirit with a chronic case of wanderlust. Without the responsibility of a husband or kids, I have this unconventional exciting existence that so many people can only dream about.

But, if you take a closer look, you'll find I'm nerdy and quirky too. Although I'm ambitious and adventurous at times, I'm also naturally guarded and cautious. I can be outgoing when necessary, but at my core, I'm an introvert. I prefer to be left alone to read books and write – until I get bored or lonely – and then I want to travel again.

I'm also a planner. I always try to plan for worst and best-case scenarios. Despite all my planning, I never planned to become a flight attendant. It was not on my long list of life goals. I kinda fell into it. Nevertheless, it has been one of the most rewarding plot twists that has allowed me to explore all the places I dreamed about, along with some I never imagined.

For my first couple of years as a flight attendant, my life was so unrecognizable that it felt as if I was really in a movie, living someone else's story. I started a blog called *Released To Crew Rest* using the pen name "Chi McFly" to document my new experiences and to make sense of it all. Plus, it was fun to share my travels with family and friends who always wanted to know about the places I went. They were understandably curious, and I was excited to talk about it. Since I've always enjoyed writing, the blog was also a great way to keep my storytelling skills sharp. Eventually, I collected so many fun stories and memorable life lessons that I knew would be of interest not just to family and friends, but also to others in the world. One day, after re-reading my old blog posts, I realized I had the framework for a book about flight attendant life from a unique perspective.

Many stories I tell in this book are lighthearted and funny. Some are a bit more serious. The book, with old blog posts sprinkled in between the happenings of my life, recounts the past seven to eight years working for a major global airline. I share some of the most memorable places I've been and the many interesting and wonderful people I've met. I write about how my occupation complicates my everyday life dealing with family, friendships, and romantic relationships. My hope is that a glimpse into a foreign world and this unconventional lifestyle will amuse and maybe even inspire you to choose your own adventure.

In all fairness, the journey, or what happens between point A and point B, has significance. There have been delays, diversions, and holding patterns in my life that has led me to the point where I am today; a place where I'm constantly evolving, learning, loving, and most importantly, laughing, even if I'm not yet "there" at my final destination.

So, here's my journey – on and off the plane. Beyond what people imagine a flight attendant's life is like and how it really is. There's the good, the bad, and the utterly embarrassing, which includes an excessive number of beach vacations along with unforgettable adventures with old and new friends.

Now, sit back and strap in as my flight attendant story begins in a turbulent state of transition...

ACT I

HOW I BECAME A
FLIGHT ATTENDANT

If you had handed me an occupational handbook with every job in the world and told me to pick my dream job, I would've skimmed right over "flight attendant." Didn't you have to be blond and skinny to do that? I'm neither. I'm tall with brown skin and curvy hips. Besides, wasn't being a flight attendant like being a waitress, janitor, or highway tollbooth worker – it's a job, not a career.

At least that's what I'd always thought. Growing up in a middle-class family in the suburbs of Detroit, I aspired to be a high-powered career woman, like a lawyer or a doctor. Maybe even a news reporter.

It wasn't until I went to college and studied abroad during my senior year did I know that travel – and more specifically, international travel – would be an important part of my professional life. After spending time in London, South Africa, and Zimbabwe, the world grew smaller and my professional

11

ambitions grew bigger. I no longer wanted to be just a career woman; I wanted to be an *international* career woman.

I didn't have to wait long. Two years after graduating from college, I moved from Detroit to Atlanta and began working with one of the city's top advertising and public relations firms. A year and a half later, at the age of twenty-five, I decided to leave and start my own business as an independent public relations consultant. I was young, ambitious, and really didn't have a clue about what I was doing, but with the help of great mentors and business partners, I figured it out.

I earned a reputation for working hard to get results fast, and soon began landing national and international clients. I worked with high-level executives, politicians and notable celebrities. I traveled all over the United States, to the Caribbean, and to Africa, assisting and managing press events for my clients. I enjoyed the thrill of racing to the airport, navigating new places, and quickly establishing the lay of the land to get the job done. Determined and driven, I was becoming the entrepreneurial mogul and career woman I had always dreamed about. In a few more years at the rate I was going, I figured I'd be flying on a private jet. In the meantime, I was a happy commercial jet-setter with enough money to buy my first home at the age of twenty-seven.

Ten years later, I was burned out. After almost a decade of being the CEO, president, vice president, administrative assistant, and head janitor of my own business, I wasn't feeling it anymore. I didn't love doing it and often found myself taking on client projects simply to pay the bills. The thrill and the challenge were gone. I was tired of always working. To make matters worse, the economy was tanking and so too were my clients' marketing budgets. The expenses of a new home and a mortgage I couldn't refinance added even more stress.

At the same time, a constant, nagging feeling that there was more to life than just accomplishing stuff scratched at my spirit. Not only was my professional life getting dull, so too was my personal life. Although I dated, there had been few serious relationships, and getting married wasn't a high priority. Building my company was more important. I was outgrowing my friends, many of whom were getting married or stuck working full-time jobs they didn't like. I wanted a more fulfilling life and was ready to do something different to get it – but I didn't know exactly what.

All I knew is I wanted more freedom to travel on my own time and dime rather than the clients'. I never really got enough time to explore the places where I worked unusually long days. I wanted better friends. Yes, I wanted to be in love with not just someone, but with life too.

After crunching numbers with my accountant and doing some soul-searching, I called it quits with the business. I let go of the three-bedroom home along with the upside-down mortgage. For the first time ever since the fourth grade, when I ruined my straight A streak by getting a B in math, I felt as if I had failed. My worst nightmare of moving back home with my mother came true as I slowly and painfully climbed out of debt. I was thirty-three years old and my plans to be a millionaire by the time I was thirty-five had fallen apart.

The first few months after I moved in with my mom were spent wandering around the house, barefoot in my bathrobe, crying, and depressed. Eventually, I pulled it together, buckled down, and started making money by writing for an online content mill. For pennies on the dollar, I researched and wrote hundreds of short articles on a wide variety of random topics ranging from how to pick the best running shoe to planning a budget wedding. Day in and day out, for over a month, I typed on the computer until I saved enough money to move out of my mother's place. I ended up renting a room in a house in the West End neighborhood of Atlanta. Renting the other room on the first floor of a two-story flat was the landlady's daughter, Anna. Anna was a flight attendant and rarely home. In her mid-to-late-twenties, she was beautiful with a witty, outgoing personality to match. On the rare occasions she was home, we'd chat it up.

One day, simply out of curiosity, I asked her about life as a flight attendant.

"Okay, so how does this flight attendant thing work? Aren't you tired of being on the go all the time?"

"Not yet. It's the best job in the world. I fly a lot at the beginning of the month to get my hours out of the way, but the beauty is that I can set my own schedule. I can fly a little or a lot."

"Wow, really? How many hours do you have to work?"

"You can work whenever. I usually work about forty hours, but next month, Damon and I are going to go check out properties in Cabo. While he's teaching his business plan class down there, I'm going to scout out a property we can buy."

Damon was Anna's boyfriend. Equally as attractive as Anna, Damon was a Yale Business School grad. Both he and Anna were involved in numerous international business ventures. I envied their partnership as an aspiring entrepreneurial power couple.

"Okay, what are the cons? How are the passengers?"

"Once in a while, you may have a whiny passenger. It's worse when you're working domestic flights, but I fly mostly international ones. On the longer flights, you feed them and they go to sleep. I get fifty dollars to pour a Coke."

"Wait, excuse me. How much?"

I heard her correctly and my eyes widened with surprise.

"In the first few years, you don't make a lot, but if you stick with it, you can pick when and where you fly."

I didn't tell Anna, but I was thinking to myself that maybe I could do this flight attendant thing. Several weeks later, Anna informed me that her company was hiring for the first time in years.

"Go on the website and apply when it opens up at midnight.

So many people apply, the website shuts down fast," she said, before running out the door to catch a flight.

At that point, I just needed a steady paycheck and something that paid more than five cents per word. I didn't know at the time that of the hundreds of thousands of people that apply to be flight attendants, only one or two percent make it to the interview round, and even fewer are hired. It was simply another possible work opportunity and I needed to apply, no matter how remote my chances were for getting the job.

THE INTERVIEW
BEFORE THE INTERVIEW

S porting a chic yet conservative wrap dress with a navy blazer, I looked like a regular business traveler catching a flight to an important meeting – or, at least I thought so. Entering the departures terminal, I confidently strode through the airport toward the security line, carrying a black slim-line tote over my left shoulder while pulling a black wheeled suitcase behind me. As instructed by Anna, I went for the classic, conservative corporate look. My hair was perfectly coiffed, thanks to a pixie-cut wig that was hiding my not-so-conservative short honey-blond dyed afro underneath. A single strand of pearls around my neck with matching earrings screamed poised, polished, and professional.

My heels were killing me and my pantyhose were itchy, but I was too excited to care. Anna warned me that my flight attendant interview began the moment I arrived at the airport.

I may not know who was watching me and when. Even though the scheduled interviews weren't until tomorrow morning, the company flew candidates out the day before. According to my interview instructions, the attire while traveling was business professional.

As I stepped into the line at the airport security checkpoint, the woman waiting in front of me glanced over her shoulder and sized me up. She wore an oversized tank top over a tube top, biker shorts, and flip-flops. It looked as if she was either heading to or just leaving the beach. She wasn't quite middle-aged and looked to be maybe in her mid-thirties, but the bags underneath her eyes made her look older. She was short and mildly stout. I couldn't tell if she was exhausted or just hungover.

"Let me guess," she said knowingly, looking up at me. "You're a flight attendant."

Pleased that I looked the part, I grinned and politely replied, "Not yet, but I'm going for an interview."

For the next twenty minutes as we stood in line, she tried to talk me out of it.

"Don't do it. It's a dead-end job," she said. "I was a flight attendant for thirty years, and now there's nothing else I can do. I don't have any real skills. No one wants to hire me. Pouring a Coke is all I know how to do."

I nodded and smiled politely while remaining silent. I gave the occasional "Mmmhmm" as if I was listening and seriously considering her advice.

This is the test, I thought. It's a test to determine how I'll deal with weird passengers that I'd rather not be talking to. Everywhere, in the terminal or on the plane, I must have my game face on at all times. She's a company plant to see if I'll lose my cool. I've dealt with clients weirder than her. I got this.

I got this. I kept saying this to myself over and over when I landed in Orlando and checked in at the hotel for the evening.

I got this as I walked into the building the next morning for a day filled with interviews.

In a large meeting room filled with nearly one hundred other candidates, I listened to a series of presentations about the company and the flight attendant positions available upon completion of training. For an hour after the presentations, we all sat quietly and upright, waiting for our turn to be escorted away for a one-on-one interview. Finally, my name was called. A tall, statuesque blond woman greeted me and led me to the interview room. I was confident but nervous at the same time as we sat down and began talking. She reviewed my resume and asked me details about my previous experience that I answered with ease as I relaxed.

"My final question. Tell me: why should we hire you?"

"I get along with all kinds of people in different environments. My prior skills, training, and experiences prepared me quite well for the position. I can handle pressure and stress while remaining professional."

Without showing a hint of approval or disapproval, she thanked me for my time and escorted me to another location. In a smaller windowless room, less than half of the original candidates sat quietly. Those in the room had advanced to the second round. The others had been dismissed. This went on for two more rounds. The questions were basically the same from each interviewer but worded differently. The personalities of the interviewers ranged from warm and friendly to reserved and unimpressed.

"Do you have any questions?" asked the second interviewer with a detached annoyance.

"Yes, what are the top qualities that will assure a candidate's success?"

"What do you think they are?" she replied back blankly.

"My best guess is someone that is focused on providing

the best customer service in tough situations," I replied with sincerity and a smile.

I got this, I repeated silently to myself, pushing away my doubts.

With the conclusion of each brief and uncertain interview, I returned to the waiting room. Each time there were fewer and fewer candidates.

At the end of a long day, my third and final interview was with a panel of interviewers who were flight attendants. There were two women and one man.

"Okay, here's the scenario," said the male interviewer. "It's late. You and your fellow crewmembers have been working all-day. On your final flight, the crew decides they're too tired and are not going through the cabin again with beverages. What do you do?"

"So, it's company policy to offer more beverages, correct?"

"Yes."

"I would remind them that it's company policy and we have to do it."

"They don't care. They're still not doing it."

"I would appeal to them again, try to empathize with being tired, but encourage them to think about the passengers."

"Nope, that doesn't work."

I paused. I didn't know the right answer.

"If they won't do it, I'd simply do it myself and make them feel really guilty for not helping," I blurted out.

The interview panelist smirked with satisfaction. The other two gave subtle nods. All three quickly thanked me as the HR coordinator walked in to lead me away. We went into her office and she closed the door.

Maybe I don't got this. I listened to my heart thumping in my chest.

She quietly studied my file as we sat down at her desk. After a few minutes, she looked up and smiled.

"Nichole, congratulations and welcome. We'd like to invite you into our flight attendant training program!"

I'M GOING
TO BE BASED WHERE?!

B rett, one of our training instructors, stepped to the front of the classroom with an excited smile on his face. A young, animated man, he dramatically clutched at his neckline with one hand as reviewed the list he was holding in his other.

"Oh my," he said, scanning the document intently.

The classroom was dead silent as all thirty-five flight attendant trainees (including myself) held our breath in anticipation, eagerly awaiting our fate.

It was the fourth week of our six-week flight attendant training program, and today, we were to receive our base location assignments. Throughout the interview process, candidates were told that if hired, and upon successful completion of training, we could be assigned to any location in the world.

Passing the interview meant that at every round of the process, you enthusiastically said you were open to such relocation. We were asked this question multiple times and in different ways. If you showed any hesitation, doubt, or uncertainty, your interview was over. You did not move on to the next round. The only correct answer to questions about relocation was an emphatic yes with as much sincerity you could muster – even if that wasn't the case.

"Are you available to start immediately?"

"Yes."

"Are you able and willing to relocate?"

"Yes."

"Would you be willing to relocate to, let's say, Antarctica if needed?"

"Absolutely!"

(But in my mind, I thought "Hell Nah!")

Once a candidate passed all three interview rounds and was invited to an upcoming training class, he or she was given a choice of ten to fifteen bases. Many but not all were located in major cities in the United States. A few were outside the United States in major international cities, but we had been informed they were not available as choices.

On the first day of class, we were instructed to rank the list of cities. Chicago was my first choice, having visited and loved the city for the first time earlier in the year. It was far enough away from Atlanta, where I resided for the past ten years. I could survive in D.C. if necessary, so that was my second choice. If I had to move out to the West Coast, my uncle lived only a few hours away from Los Angeles. If I got any of my other lower-ranked choices, I'd have to reconsider this whole flight attendant thing. At that time when we were ranking our choices, none of us knew (or those that knew didn't tell us) that only half of the U.S. bases were open and accepting new-hire flight attendants. Okay, now back to the story:

"This is quite unexpected," said the instructor, pausing once again and now studying the list a bit too hard.

Throwing his hands in the air and flinging his head back in Oprah gift-giving fashion, he screamed, "Congratulations! Everyone in the class is going to *Loooondooooon*!"

Jaws dropped as the news sank in. Living the exciting life of an internationally based flight attendant straight out of training class was beyond our wildest dreams. After the shock, the classroom erupted into cheers. We hugged each other with bewildered tears of joy in our eyes. There was an overflow of excited chatter and electrifying energy. Okay, London wasn't on my list – it wasn't on anyone's list – but I could make it work!

After a few minutes, the instructor shushed the class and patiently waited for everyone to calm down before continuing with more details. A mischievous smile slowly spread across his face before he burst out laughing.

"April Fool's! I'm just kidding!"

In the back of the room, the other trainers chuckled at his prank.

"That one never gets old!" Brett proclaimed as he struggled to catch his breath between his fits of laughter.

We all groaned with disappointment while we tried to put our hearts back into our chests. It wasn't even April! It was January!

"Many of you got either your first, second, or third choice. To those of you who didn't get the base you wanted, just know that it's not permanent. You can transfer after six months to any of the other open bases."

One by one, he called our names and announced our assigned base.

I got my first choice: I was heading to Chicago O'Hare International Airport.

◆ ◆ ◆ ◆ ◆

If Antarctica had been on the list, I might as well have picked it because Antarctica is exactly what Chicago looked like on the day I landed in late February of 2014 for base orientation. It looked nothing like the city I fell in love with during my visits, which, in hindsight, had been in the spring and summer months.

The last time I visited Chicago was around Memorial Day weekend in 2010, right before my financial downturn. I took a few days off and road-tripped from Atlanta to Chicago with my two older cousins. We goofed off at Navy Pier, then wandered the shops on 53rd Street in Hyde Park. I decided, while devouring a bag of Garrett's popcorn, that Chicago, home to history-making politicians and mobsters, would eventually be my home too. How or when I would move to this great city were details I would eventually figure out. At that time, the flight attendant opportunity was not even on my radar. I just knew that I liked the Chicago vibe and had outgrown the slow, southern pace of Atlanta.

Born and raised in Michigan, I always hated winter. Before the age of ten, I vowed that as soon as I turned eighteen, I was gone. When I was trying to figure out where to go to college, weather was a huge consideration. Less important was the quality of the school; if there was sunshine more often than there was snow, I applied. Schools in Georgia, Texas, California, and Florida were at the top of my list. But, for my parents, who were paying for the bulk of my college tuition, cost was their biggest consideration. I ended up going to school in state. I spent five more years in Michigan, trekking through snow and never being warm enough.

In 2001, three months after college graduation, I finally escaped Michigan. As fall turned to winter during my first year in Atlanta, the sun was still shining! A fleece pullover and maybe a hat is all I needed to get me through the season. On the rare occasions of snow, I found it amusing that the entire city would shut down. When I left a few minutes early for work on a snowy day, I drove fifteen minutes to the office to find that everyone else stayed home due to inclement weather. I couldn't believe with fewer than two inches of white stuff on the ground, kids in Georgia got to stay home. In Michigan, you'd be hard-pressed to get a day off if there was a foot of snow!

I think it was the warm weather, low cost of living, and the fact that her only two children lived there is what eventually led my mother, a retired teacher, to relocate to Atlanta. She found an apartment on her own and moved herself down a year or two later, before my dad and stepmother also bought a summer home in Atlanta. There was no longer a need for me to ever travel to Michigan except for an occasional funeral or a wedding. Behind me were the bitter, cold memories of icy sidewalks, snow that turned to slush, and hands numbed to the point of nearly falling off, despite wearing two pairs of gloves. I finally broke off my relationship with Midwest winters for good. I could start to build a life that revolved around warmth and summer.

But ten years later, I somehow found myself back in snot-freezing cold and Lawd knows, I wasn't ready for it. I didn't even own a real winter coat anymore! It was hard for me to accept that I'd voluntarily chosen to live in Chicago. During my decision-making process, my mind just didn't register that Chicago was only a five-hour drive from that vaguely familiar place called Detroit and it too was a city on a lake! Not only was it cold but it was windy too! Brett's advice that we could put in for transfer after six months gave me comfort along with my plan to temporarily escape Chicago winter as often as I could in the meantime.

Yeah, that's what I'll do...I'll fly away to warmer weather at every chance I get.

However, at the present moment, I was stuck.

To make matters worse, in the middle of winter, I had yet to find a place to live in Chicago. I graduated from flight attendant training on a Friday in Orlando and was scheduled for base orientation on Wednesday. In other words, I had five days to get back from Orlando to Atlanta, unpack and repack from six weeks of hotel-living (with a roommate), and then head off to Chicago. Although I received my base assignment during training, the twelve-hour days of classroom training, night-studying, and tests every two days left little time to investigate Chicago from afar.

But I wasn't too worried. Anna, who was based in New York but commuted from Atlanta, made it seem as if finding a place would be easy. She mentioned that flight attendant crash pads near the airport were often posted on a bulletin board in the base's employee break room that I could check out when I arrived. Along with six weeks of hotel accommodations during training, the company paid for two additional nights in our assigned city during base orientation. After that, we were on our own with finding someplace to stay between trips.

My starting hourly wage (far from fifty dollars an hour) and credit score wouldn't be enough to afford my own apartment right away. For the next few years, my annual income as a reserve flight attendant would barely put me above the poverty line. But it would be steady income and I planned to take on freelance marketing jobs whenever I could. Most flight attendants had family or friends in the assigned cities where they planned to live. While I had cousins that lived in Chicago, they lived too far from O'Hare airport, and if I lived with them, I'd have to take a train and a bus for at least two hours each way, which wouldn't work. I didn't have a reliable car that would even survive the trek from Atlanta to Chicago. With newly minted flight privileges, I left my car behind at my mom's house and flew from Atlanta to Chicago to begin my new job.

◆ ◆ ◈ ◆ ◆

Once I touched down in Chicago, I located the board with crash pad vacancies to discover there were only a few postings. When I called, they were already taken. The one place I checked out was a dusty one-bedroom apartment. Although it was only two train stops away from the airport, I couldn't bring myself to stay in a place with four bunk beds and a pullout sofa in the living room for six male and two female flight attendants in their twenties. Did you do the math? Exactly. I did my time in crowded dorms during college with roommates from hell and was certain that despite my limited funds, I could find something better.

But, on the next day at the conclusion of orientation and the last night in a company-paid hotel room, temperatures dropped to a single digit, accompanied by a below-freezing wind chill and six inches of snow. Using public transportation, trudging around unfamiliar neighbors in the evening after an all-day orientation was impossible.

At 11 a.m., one hour before check-out time, the reality of my situation started to sink in. Here I was, in a new city, with a new job, but no place to go. It would be at least a few hours before I could check into another and cheaper hotel. My mood was as glum as the gray skies outside my hotel window.

The situation was far from dire – it was just overwhelming. There was the excitement about getting the interview, going to training, the stress of training to get hired, and then relocating fast. I had been existing in constant states of anticipation and uncertainty about everything for such a long time. So many life changes were now happening all at once and happening so quickly. Plus, I was still reeling from the past two years that had been emotionally overwhelming and mentally exhausting. In

Atlanta, I was always on the go: moving out of my home, to my mother's place, and then to renting a room in the city. I constantly chased new opportunities, trying to do something different. Many of my attempts failed and bouncing back repeatedly from disappointment after disappointment took its toll.

The resources that I had in the past were now limited. I didn't have the money, the network, or even the confidence that I once had to just make things happen. It felt as if I was trying to weave together this new life with one hand tied behind my back. It was beyond frustrating. In fact, I wasn't even sure yet if this flight attendant thing would work out and if it was what I really wanted. Although Chicago was now my home, I was far from settled.

I sat on the edge of the hotel bed, thinking about all of this. I was bummed about my predicament as well as a bit scared and lonely with no one to talk to. It was the middle of the day. My cousins were at work. My few friends back home were at work. My mom was so excited that I had gotten a job, I couldn't call her to whine. Plus, I was just plain cold despite turning the thermostat in the hotel room all the way up. The frost on the windows and piles of snow outside made everything much worse.

Without any friends to call and invite, the only ones to show up at my pity party were my loneliness, doubts, fears, and regrets. I thought about how sucky the weather was. The sucky crash pad I saw. My sucky roommate during training that I hoped I'd never have to fly with. I thought about the fact that I should have more money and the jobs I worked that didn't pay enough.

And then I cried.

After a good twenty minutes of feeling sorry for myself, I felt better. My pity party was over. But, my doubts and fears lingered and just would not leave. They were kind of like those last hangers-on at a real party. The ones that don't get the hint;

even though you thanked them for coming, they're still sitting on your damn sofa.

So, rather than ignore my doubts and fears, I began addressing them one by one. The conversation with myself went something like this:

Me: *I have no place to go.*

Also Me: Calm down. In a few hours, you will check into a cheaper hotel. What you have is time to kill before check-in at another place.

Me: *I have nothing to do.*

Also Me: Go meet people.

Me: *It's cold outside. I don't know anyone or where to go.*

Also Me: Really, you don't know anyone else in Chicago? What about that guy Mike you met a few years ago?

Me: *He probably doesn't even remember me. I don't know if I still have his number.*

Also Me: Look woman, you have nothing to lose and absolutely nothing to do!

Without thinking about too much more about it, I dialed Mike's number, expecting to get his voice mail.

Me: *He's probably at work too like everyone else.*

I met Mike for the first time during my last visit to Chicago over three years ago. I posted an online ad on Craigslist, looking for someone to hang out with on the Sunday night before Memorial Day. This was pre- "serial killers on Craigslist" days (I think). My cousins and I had been hanging out all weekend. They were recovering from our previous nights of partying in the city and weren't up to going back out on Sunday. I wanted to go out, but not by myself. So, being the creative problem-solver that

I was, I posted an ad in the "Platonic Women Seeking Men" section of Craigslist:

> SBF, 33, in town visiting and looking for a cool guy to hang out with. I'm not looking to hook up, just to have a good time in the city. You must be normal. No weirdos. Send pic. No pic no reply.

Having bought and sold things on Craigslist and dated online in the era of MySpace and BlackPlanet, I was a pro at being specific, straightforward, and cautious with online interactions.

After sifting through a flood of replies ranging from a little weird to flat-out creepy, I came across a normal response from a normal, even cute-looking guy named Mike, age thirty-three. In his picture, he had a black buzz cut along with a friendly smile and dark eyes that, most importantly, said "I'm sane." In his short reply, Mike was looking for something to do as well and was interested in hanging out. Like me, he liked reading, travel, and politics.

Mike and I met up at a jazz club downtown that my cousins recommended. He looked like his picture (which was a relief) and turned out to be a cool, down-to-earth guy. If he liked me, he played it cool, and thankfully didn't show it. I wasn't interested in a date. I already had too much going on in life. Nevertheless, we had a good time talking about the best cities to visit, our favorite authors and our least favorite politicians. We agreed that if he ever stopped through Atlanta, I would definitely return the favor and show him around. My mission to make a new friend and have a good night out had been accomplished.

When I called Mike on that cold day in February as a new flight attendant, it had been over a year since we last sent the other a "Hello, just keeping in touch" text. We never really talked on the phone. After our first meeting, life for me became so chaotic and focused around finding work; keeping in touch with anyone was low on the list of life priorities (unless they were hiring).

Surprised yet happy to hear from me, Mike instantly remembered me. He sounded like the same cool, down-to-earth guy I had met a few years back. Although my nose was still stuffy from sniffling, I tried to sound happy and as if I hadn't been crying a few minutes before.

"Yeah, so I live in Chicago now," I said casually when he asked what I'd been up to. "I just got a job as a flight attendant!"

"Wow, congratulations!"

"Thanks! I start tomorrow and I'm off today."

"Cool, I'm off-work too today. Want to go to lunch? Where are you? I'll come pick you up."

Just like that, my day and mood instantly shifted. Now with someplace to go and something to do, I headed to the lobby to check out and wait for Mike. He picked me up in his red 1990 Toyota Celica and we went out to lunch. I told him all about my flight attendant training and my search for a place to live between trips. He told me about the different neighborhoods and the best areas for flight attendants.

"Well, if you want, you can stay with me while you look. I live in Pilsen, but it's a bit far from the airport."

I appreciated his offer, but politely declined. Mike was a cool guy, but I still didn't know him that well. I wasn't about to stay with some stranger I met from Craigslist only to find out in the middle of the night that he's a serial killer. And miss my first day at work because I'm dead? Nope, I wasn't going out like that!

After lunch, Mike drove me around to different areas, looking at places for rent that were between the city and the airport. I was so thankful to not have to trek around town by foot in the snow. I didn't find anything that afternoon but was encouraged by the possibilities. In the evening, Mike dropped me off at the airport. Nervous about getting to the airport on time should I get called in the middle of the night, I decided to stay at that Hilton attached to the airport. Even with my new corporate employee discount, it was still pricey, but I could afford one night.

Later that evening after getting settled in, I checked my schedule on the computer. As informed during training, new flight attendants were expected to log into a portal at a designated time each evening to check their schedule for an assignment. If we were not yet assigned a trip, we would simply sit around and wait for a phone call from crew scheduling, which could be anytime that evening, in the middle of the night, or sometime the next day.

When I logged in on the computer, I had an assignment for the next day waiting – a three-day trip starting at 5 a.m. Three days meant two nights in a hotel room that I didn't have to pay for myself. The icing on the cake was that my layovers would be in Miami on the first night and then Cancun the next.

STEVE URKEL OF THE AIR

When I imagined what my first day of work as a flight attendant would be like, I saw myself as this glamorous Naomi Campbell look-alike (except a little bit thicker), strutting through the airport from one flight to the next. I'd be laughing it up and chatting with my equally attractive crewmembers while flinging my perfect waist-length weave away from my flawlessly made-up face. On the aircraft, I would be a cross between Martha Stewart and B. Smith, serving up gourmet cuisine from the galley. God forbid, if all hell broke loose, I would channel Lynda Carter and go Wonder Woman, sans lasso and gold boots.

But, on my first day of work, I was more like Steve Urkel. The only thing I flung was a carton of mushroom soup that landed everywhere in the galley except in the bowl.

Oooooh, did I doooo thaaaat? is what I was thinking but didn't say to my coworker Crystal as she wiped the glob of

33

mushroom soup that was dripping from her hair into her face. Thoroughly mortified, I apologized profusely.

"That's okay," she said quietly and then breathed deeply.

Along with being beautiful, Crystal, who was working in the front galley with me, was a Jedi at keeping her composure. Her patience with the clueless, clumsy new hire was endless.

During training, we spent forty one and a half of forty two days on aircraft security and safety procedures and the other half-day on food service protocols. Although I had waitressed before getting the flight attendant gig, I hadn't been a very good at it. Even during training, I had little interest in learning the difference between a rocks glass and a champagne flute.

My inattention to food service during training was evident on my randomly assigned position as the front-galley flight attendant. Prepping the meals for twenty first-class passengers in the tiniest kitchen ever was new territory for me. I could tell you the location of the fire extinguishers and how to properly put on a life vest, but I couldn't find the potholders and extra napkins that were also stored on the plane. While Crystal went into the lavatory to clean herself off, I wiped up the mushroom soup that had splattered all over the galley floor and flight deck door. The hungry first-class passengers would have to wait a few more minutes.

As far as strutting from terminal to terminal, it was more like hobbling and jogging. I was hobbling because the new black heels I had bought for work were not made for walking long distances on hard surfaces. My feet were throbbing before takeoff during my first flight. Fumbling to get my luggage together after passengers exited, I was the last of my crew to get off the plane on every leg. Since I didn't have a clue about how to navigate the airports, I frequently jogged off the plane up the jet bridge to catch up with everyone as we headed to our next flight. All the while, I clumsily dragged my over-packed bags with one hand and my in-flight flats in the other.[1] My company-issued purse kept slipping off my shoulder and slowed me down even more. So much for Naomi Campbell.

The passengers themselves were uneventful. I nervously said "hi" as they boarded. Fortunately, since I was cooking in the galley, I had very little interaction with most passengers during the flight unless it involved refilling a glass or being handed an empty tray.

We arrived in Miami that night with a short, nine-hour layover at an unimpressive airport hotel. Climbing out of the property's shuttle van after a five-minute ride, we each wheeled our luggage into the plainly decorated lobby that smelled of stale chlorine and dust. To the right of the entrance was a small sitting area furnished with fake palm plants and pleather lounge chairs. To the left was a hotel clerk, slouching on a stool behind a laminate front desk counter. The clerk looked as tired as we felt and had already lined our room keys up on the counter for a speedy check-in.

To celebrate, the crew took me out to a quick dinner at the hotel restaurant since we all had to get up before dawn. With their help and encouragement, I survived my first day. One of the flight attendants gave me her extra shoe bag as a welcome present so I could store my flats.

By the second day on the plane, I was getting the hang of things. It wasn't until we arrived in Cancun early afternoon with a sixteen-hour layover that I finally exhaled. After a twenty-minute van drive, we checked into another Hilton that was much different from our previous layover hotel. The hotel bellhop greeted us at the entrance and promptly proceeded to unload our luggage as another bellhop ushered us into an expansive lobby

---

1   Flight attendants are allowed to wear flats after takeoff during the flight but must change back to shoes upon landing prior to exiting the aircraft.

with vaulted ceilings, marble tiled floors, and stone columns. There were multiple sitting areas with groups of gorgeous leather chairs and sofas. In one corner, a huge vase of exotic fresh flowers sat atop a black baby grand piano that, although absent of a pianist, piped soft classical melodies throughout the lobby. Four clerks working the front desk counter checked us in simultaneously while informing us of the available amenities.

My room was equally impressive. Anchored by a posh king-sized bed, it was tastefully decorated with hard-carved wooden furniture. I opened the window shutters to discover that the balcony in my room overlooked a pool nestled between an array of tropical plants and flowers. This was more like it! Behind the bathroom door was a plush, oversized bathrobe and slippers. Hand-carved soaps sat atop a stack of thick, fluffy towels. I couldn't believe this was the start of my new life!

After a luxurious nap on Egyptian cotton sheets and a mound of fluffy white pillows, I spent the late afternoon lounging by the pool and working out in the fitness center with every machine imaginable. I met up with the crew in the lobby and we went to a restaurant nearby for dinner later that evening. With fewer than twenty-four hours, there wasn't really time to venture too far from the hotel. I didn't dare explore the city alone and risk getting lost – or even worse, missing my next flight!

THERE'S NO PLACE LIKE HOME (OR IS THERE?)

T hree days and six flights later, I returned to Chicago beyond exhausted. My work days were almost thirteen hours each day, with morning-report times as early as 4 and 5 a.m.[2] Coming down from all the excitement and nervousness of the past few days, I just wanted to go to bed. I still didn't have any place to live or any energy to figure it out. It was early in the evening, so I headed through the terminal to the employee crew room to nap before looking for a cheaper airport hotel.

Checking my voice mail as I walked through the terminal, there was a message from Mike. We hadn't talked since he took

2   Report time is the time at which flight attendants have to be on the plane
     to prepare for boarding and departure which is usually about an hour
     before the flight is scheduled to leave.

me out to lunch before my first day, which now felt like months ago rather than a few days. Before we departed that day, Mike promised to keep an eye out if he came across a room or crash pad. His voice mail mentioned that he may have found a place that would be a fit for me.

"I checked with my dad and his girlfriend and they said you can stay there while you look for a place," he said when I called him back.

Again, although Mike was cool, I didn't know him too well, let alone his family. But, at that point, I hadn't even thought about a place to stay while I was gone. If his family was renting a room, maybe it was within my budget and could be a temporary solution.

Born and raised in Chicago, Mike's family was originally from Mexico. Although I knew Mike had his own place in Pilsen, I assumed that the rest of his close-knit extended family lived together, like in many of Atlanta's Mexican-immigrant communities. I remembered when I lived in Michigan, I had an older cousin that had a lot of Mexican friends. If Mike's folks were anything like my cousin's friends (who were the only Mexicans I knew and not that well), there would be used cars under repair in the yard and banda music playing all the time. In reality though, I had no idea where his folks lived or how they lived, which concerned me the most. Since I was new to Chicago and the area, finding a relatively safe and comfortable place was important. But, at this point, I was open to the possibility of a place other than the employee lounge to sleep.

Mike picked me up again (this time, from baggage claim) and we drove over to his folks' place. They lived in Logan square near the blue line 'L' station that went straight to the airport, which was a good sign. We drove through the tree-lined peaceful neighborhood. Pulling up to the location, a wooden fence obscured the two-story house from the street. *That's probably to conceal all the cars in the yard*, I thought foolishly to myself. *Makes sense.*

But, when he opened the gate, there weren't any cars. Just a small, snow-covered patio with a walkway leading to the front door.

Without knocking, Mike walked into the house and I followed. We stepped into the living room straight out of a Pottery Barn winter catalog. There was a cozy sofa with pillows in front of an electric fireplace that was emitting a warm orange glow. A complementing posh recliner with a perfectly draped throw blanket was situated in the corner. Chatter and the aroma of food coming from the kitchen pulled us farther into the house. We followed the voices to find smiling faces sitting around a quaint dining table greeting us.

Mike introduced me to everyone before hanging our coats in the hallway closet. There were Mike's folks, Marsha and Miguel, along with a young blonde woman named Shona. We joined everyone at the kitchen table. They were as eager to hear details about my new job as I was to share. They asked me questions about my first trip as Miguel stood at the stove, preparing food. Savory warm fragrances of mushrooms, herbs, and spices wafted from the pots.

Although excited to meet everyone, I was overwhelmed with so many new sights and sounds all at once. I was struggling to take it all in. The beautifully decorated and brightly-lit kitchen. The colorful, intriguing pieces of art hung alongside family portraits on the walls. The refrigerator door adorned with a child's crayon drawings.

I talked about my nervousness and excitement of the past few days with ease, as if I was chatting with my own family. Miguel, a tall, older man with curly salt and pepper hair and black-rimmed glasses, listened thoughtfully before interrupting with questions. With equal intensity, I concentrated on understanding his words that he spoke slowly with a thick, Mexican accent. Marsha, a petite Jewish white woman, reminded me of my own mother. With blue-framed glasses perched atop her head, she even had a teacher vibe like my mother. Marsha's voice reminded me of an Italian New Yorker except much quieter. I was not surprised when she told me she was retired from the education field. Shona, a visiting family friend and college exchange student from London, spoke in a clipped, distinctly British accent.

All the while as we chatted, I was hungry, sleepy, and still thawing out from the cold. Nevertheless, I was determined to stay engaged as the center of everyone's attention while we enjoyed a delicious dinner of warm tortillas filled with cheese, avocados, and fresh vegetables. It was the first home-cooked meal I had eaten in months.

An hour later, I was content and full as delirium began to set in. I wanted so bad to lay my head on my empty plate and fall asleep listening to everyone else talk. I had yet to see the room and could care less if it was simply a storage closet. I wanted to stay here with Marsha, Miguel, and Shona.

"How much for the room?" I discreetly asked Marsha, who sat next to me at the table.

She shrugged her shoulders. "I hadn't thought about that. Just get some rest and we can figure it out. You can stay in the room my granddaughter stays in when she comes to visit."

Eager to square away a place to stay, I was equally content with her suggestion to just rest. I was so grateful for a comfortable, safe place.

After dinner, I followed Mike to the car to grab my stuff. I couldn't thank him enough for introducing me to his folks. I still was perplexed by their generosity. I wondered if perhaps they thought I was Mike's new girlfriend.

"Mike, do your folks think we're dating or something?"

"No, I told them I met you on Craigslist."

It wasn't until days later that I realized Marsha and Miguel didn't have a room to rent. They were simply opening their home to me – a stranger from Craigslist that also happened to be a homeless flight attendant.

HIGHLIGHTS OF CHI-LIFE

Neither Shona nor I approved of Glenn's choice to investigate the disturbance alone.

"I don't think that's a very wise decision on his part," Shona firmly declared. Her British accent still amused me. I loved listening to her speak.

"I know, right?" I said, shaking my head in disbelief.

"Glenn, come on! Don't do it!" I desperately shouted, knowing he wouldn't listen.

Marsha, Shona, and I cringed as we watched Glenn step around the dark corner of an abandoned convenience store to discover a pack of disfigured corpses, huddled over their meal of human flesh. Blood was dripping from their gnarled faces. Terrified, Glenn foolishly stumbled back, knocking over a shelf of canned goods and marking himself as the zombie's next kill.

He was saved by a Tide commercial. With the episode almost over, we were hopeful that he would survive for at least another week.

"This is too gruesome for me. I'm turning in," Marsha said, getting up from the recliner. Shona and I laughed and wished her goodnight. The two of us stayed huddled together on the sofa under blankets in the basement den to watch the rest of *The Walking Dead* without her. Marsha headed upstairs to join Miguel, who had retired to bed an hour earlier.

I'd been working for the airlines and living with Marsha, Miguel, and Shona for almost three weeks. I was in and out of town most days, but on the occasions when I was in Chicago, watching TV in the downstairs den after dinner with Shona and Marsha became the evening routine. While the three of us chatted it up between commercials, we could often hear Miguel upstairs, bustling around and listening to cable news on the small TV in the kitchen.

The extreme temperatures that welcomed me to Chicago persisted, followed by ice, then more snow, making it difficult to get around the city. With early-morning work assignments on most days, I frequently left the house well before sunrise. Tiptoeing around to get dressed, I bundled up and ventured out into the dark cold, wheeling my luggage to the nearby 'L' station. It was eerily quiet in the mornings, but the neighborhood felt safe. Besides, no one would be lurking around in the extreme temperatures unless they had to.

I'd come back to Marsha and Miguel's usually a day or two later in the late afternoon or early evenings. Just like the first day, exhausted and hungry, my return welcome would be as warm as my first arrival. I was as happy to see them as they were me. Miguel (sometimes Marsha) would cook, and I could never resist good food and conversation. After changing out of my work uniform, I'd stay at the kitchen table, chatting as long as I could before going to crash in the upstairs bedroom. It always felt as if I had been gone for months rather than just a few days, and it was always was like catching up with family I hadn't seen in years. On the rare occasion I was home during the day or on a weekend, family, friends, or neighbors would often stop over to visit. I'd meet Marsha's son, daughter-in-law, the granddaughter who was too young to care that I occupied her room, Miguel's nieces and nephews, and Shona's friends. Mike stopped by occasionally to do his laundry. All of us gathered around the kitchen table. We would eat, laugh, and drink while talking about Obama's latest fight with the Republicans, new art exhibits coming to Chicago and funny stories from our past. Our conversations were always dynamic as we talked about our lives, our different cultures, and current events.

On my off days, usually after long trips, I'd sleep until the middle of the day. I'd find Marsha sitting at the kitchen table reading or surfing the web while Miguel prepared a meal. Eager to have a new guest to serve, Miguel always offered me a glass of whatever he was drinking, which was usually a craft beer.

"Hi, Nichole!" he'd say cheerfully. "Are you hungry?"

After eating at airports and restaurant hotels, my answer was always yes. If there was no food prepared, he would quickly begin cooking.

"Want a beer?"

Not a beer drinker, I would always decline. He'd then ask me if I wanted wine as he proudly showed me the wide variety of wine and liquor in the cabinets beneath the counter.

On days I was on duty, I'd settle on tea and coffee. Subtle disappointment would register across his face. It was quirky and amusing. After getting home from a trip, I'd always chat over a drink longer than I had planned before eventually going to bed. With Miguel, a retired professional artist, I'd talk about religion, aliens, and art. With Marsha, I talked about practical matters of the places I was looking to stay and the happenings during my travels. With an informal arrangement that felt like a family adoption, Marsha never gave me a price for rent, but

I paid her what I could with a promise to find a place as soon as I could. Like the mom that she was, Marsha encouraged me to take my time looking for a place. I was so grateful for their unexpected hospitality and wanted to be mindful that I didn't overstay my welcome. It was four of us in the three-bedroom home, but it was never crowded. It was just home.

By spring, as Chicago thawed out, Shona headed back to London, and I found a permanent place to stay. Between trips while on crew rest, I visited them frequently. With warmer weather, the three of us migrated from their kitchen table to the outside front patio. The sky smelled of flowers and fresh cut grass. The towering tree branches keeping watch over the patio that were bare in the winter became peppered with small, budding lime green leaves, promising an abundance of shade for the summer. Perennials and shrubs, instead of snow, adorned the patio along with bistro tables, lounge chairs, and recliners. During the spring in the equally cozy outdoor space, I'd stop by to find Marsha tending to the patio garden while Miguel read or napped in a lounger. We'd sometimes walk to one of the nearby restaurants and talk about how much we missed Shona. As everyone ventured outside again, the quiet winter neighborhood was now bustling with joggers, dog walkers and yard sales.

The permanent space I found was a private basement room in a three-story multi-family home within walking distance from Marsha and Miguel's house. A woman named Debbie responded to a Craigslist ad I posted in search of a room. The room as described fit my location requirements (walking distance to the 'L') and small budget. The outside of the home was in need of a new coat of paint. It was one of the older, not-yet-rehabbed, rental homes on the block that were mixed in with a handful of recently rehabbed and newly constructed homes.

The room was tiny, but furnished with a desk, dresser, and bed. There was a spacious shared kitchen, and most importantly, the place was spotless. Debbie, a middle-aged divorcée with short red hair, shared that in her spare time, she enjoyed cleaning and housekeeping. I was the first of three tenants to move into the smallest of the basement rooms that she was subleasing. After a flood a few months back, the basement had been renovated by the owner and sectioned off into three rooms with plywood doors.

"I think the plumbing issue is fixed, but make sure everything is off the floor," she cautioned. "You may want to get renters insurance."

I was uncertain and nervous as to who the other occupants would be. These rooms were inexpensive considering the area. Debbie had shared with me stories of her previous tenants, one of whom was a raging alcoholic who she had to finally evict.

"If you know of anyone, send them my way," she said.

Over the weeks, as I flew with other new flight attendants, I met a few who were in the same situation as I had been and were looking for an affordable crash pad. On different flights, I became friends with Linda, a flight attendant who commuted from Houston, and Rose, who commuted from St. Louis but planned to eventually relocate to Chicago. I told them about where I lived and the month-to-month rental flexibility. Each ended up renting one of the other two larger rooms. None of us were home much. On rare occasions, all three of us were on crew rest[3] and in town at the same time. We'd lounge around and chat. Every now and then, we went out together to the Wicker Park bars.

By late spring, Linda and Rose moved out. They had each found apartments with other flight attendants. Wanting my

---

3   Crew rest is the time between assigned work trips which usually ranges from ten hours to a couple of days.

own room, but without an apartment price, I stayed in the smaller, cheaper room. I was anxious and nervous again about my replacement roommates.

Both Debbie and I preferred more flight attendants but she ended up renting to guys who responded to her ads. The first new tenant was Yusef, a graphic designer in his late twenties who recently moved from Poland. Yusef was quiet, clean, and kept to himself.

About a month later, Brad from Minneapolis moved in. He was the exact opposite of Yusef. Brad was in his early twenties but acted as if he was nineteen. He talked on and on about nothing of importance. In my opinion, he was a typical frat boy bro, but worse than that, he smelled like sweat all the time. He often left the kitchen and bathroom a mess. When the guys moved in, Debbie wisely understood the hygiene habits of men would be a problem for me and suggested that she and I share the spacious upstairs bathroom. The guys would use the smaller one downstairs.

At the peak of summer travel, from May until August, I was rarely home enough to be concerned with either of the guys. Most of my days were spent in airports, on planes, and at layover hotels. Between trips in Chicago, I usually lounged around in my room and slept, trying to recover from the previous trip or prepare for the next.

Debbie's basement was nowhere near as cozy as Marsha and Miguel's. It indeed felt like a crash pad without the other flight attendants. But, the twin bed was comfortable enough. Except for the occasional door slamming followed by the shuffling feet up the stairs, I didn't see or hear my roommates too much when I was home. In early mornings and evenings, I'd occasionally run into Debbie, who also worked early mornings until the evening at her two jobs. A homebody when she wasn't working, she was cool to talk to, although most of her time was spent in her room with her boyfriend, Dave. During most of the day, the place was usually empty. It was just me and Tux, Debbie's anti-social cat. We'd lounge around, staying out of each other's way.

Although life was far from normal, I was now settled into a space of my own with a bit of a steady income. I was happier than I had been in a while. The job was still exciting and new. I felt as if I was once again getting back on track with life – this time, a bit wiser and a lot more grateful.

BLOG POST:
OOOH, YOU'RE A FLIGHT ATTENDANT

Chi Mc Fly | May 21, 2014 | Released To Crew Rest

"What do you do?"

Even before I was a flight attendant, I didn't like asking or answering that question. Especially at business networking events where people try to size you up to determine what they can do for you, or what you can do for them. But now, at events when I'm out meeting new people, strangers, upon knowing what I do, get excited, curious, and sometimes envious. If I allow it, the conversation then goes on and on about my occupation. I'm peppered with nonstop questions.

When I first started, I didn't mind. In fact, I liked talking about my job. It was new for me too and I was excited to share.

But after a few months, the conversations were predictable with the same follow-up questions all the time. It usually went like this:

Me: I'm a flight attendant.

Them: Ooooh! What airline do you work for?

I respond that I work for *redacted.* Following my response is their personal airline horror story that I didn't ask for.

And then it's back to more questions: How do you like it? What's your normal route? Do you travel internationally? Do you get to fly for free? Do they pay for your hotel? Oh boy, I bet you have some crazy passenger stories.

Then they wait for me to tell them a few stories to keep them entertained. If I'm not in the mood, I lie and say "Not really."

The conversation and questions vary only slightly depending on the demographics. If it's an older woman, after telling me she always wanted to be a flight attendant, she unabashedly asks me if I'm married with kids. In their minds, being single is the only way a person can live a life of travel, although I know a lot of flight attendants who are married with kids. If it's a younger woman, she asks how does "someone" get to be a flight attendant and if my company is hiring.

If it's a man, whether they're flirting or not (often, they are), they think that all flight attendants have multiple lovers, boyfriends, or husbands in different cities. They are always curious to know about The Mile-High Club...

The most obnoxious of strangers will ask, "Oooh, what's up with the buddy passes?" Let's get this straight right now: buddy passes are for buddies. Key word, buddy. As in someone I actually know, not random strangers or friends-of-a-friend who I just met two minutes ago. Fun fact: flight attendants who sell buddy passes for profit actually risk losing their jobs.

I try to be polite when such conversations arise, but it's gotten to be annoying – especially when I'm tired or just trying to mind my business between flights. I don't mind sharing details of my life with people I know. But strangers, not so much. Especially when I'm just getting off work. Just because I'm in uniform, the last thing I want to talk about is work to a random stranger sitting next to me on the bus.

I get it. Many people are curious. From the outside looking in, flight attendant life is glamorous and exciting. A lot of people dream about the freedom to travel to new places frequently and still earn a living. Many people can't do so because of limited resources like time and money. In all honesty, flight attendant life can be exciting, but glamorous, not so much. Despite all the benefits, it's still a job that requires hard work.

Most people still have this misconception about flight attendant life based on outdated ideals from the 1960s, when being in aviation actually was glamorous. You had to be single, unmarried, young, attractive, and petite to fit into those chic, fashionable uniforms. Airline ads featured sexy, alluring flight attendants catering to upper-class white male business travelers. Movies like *Catch Me If You Can* and *Pam Am* depict flight attendant life as one of wild parties, drugs, and sex with the pilots. Maybe it was like that at one time, but not now.

Workforces, workplaces, and customers in all U.S. industries (aviation included) have changed with the times. As more people travel, this includes more working-class and middle-class families. Airlines that once catered only to upper-middle-class and male business travelers now compete with discount air carriers and have some of everybody on the same plane. Different carriers cater to different types of travelers, but for irresistible flight deals, research shows that even the most loyal customers will jump ship and fly another airline.

The biggest transformation of the airline industry was 9/11. Not only did this event transform the entire industry, but it also presented a sobering reality of just how challenging our jobs as flight attendants can be. As the industry spiraled after the tragic events, flight attendants' responsibilities expanded, especially in the areas of safety and security. Drunks on a plane were no longer our biggest safety threat. Along with stricter security measures in the airport terminals, flight attendants also faced the wrath of stressed-out passengers boarding the plane.

I wasn't working as a flight attendant in 2001, but when I talk with those who were, they often say that flight attendant life is more grueling now. The workdays are longer, the pay is less, and the layovers are shorter. The older ones reminisce about the days when crews stuck together on layovers and had so much fun. There was stronger camaraderie and better passenger service. I remember the time when meals were served in economy class on domestic flights.

But, the stereotypes about flight attendant life persist among the general public for the most part, thanks to the media. Reports about drunken flight attendants, drunken pilots and World–Star–worthy airplane fights get as much attention as an airline crash, which makes all these incidents seem commonplace. Like anything involving sex and violence, happenings on a plane are often glamorized, sensationalized, and exaggerated. It doesn't mean that there's not some truth to the stories you hear in the news, but usually, what's shared in the media and how it's shared is not the full story.

At the end of the day, flight attending is what I do (thus I'm turning it into a verb); it's not who I am. I learned from my previous job as a consultant that tying my identity to what I do for a living can be dangerous. Because when it changes, whether by choice or not, you risk not knowing who you are anymore. So, although I really like my job, I am not my job. It takes effort to ensure that it's not all-consuming.

LAYOVER LIFE: THE PLACES I WENT, THE SLEEP I DIDN'T GET

My second layover in Cancun was about ten months after my first one. This time, it was on Christmas Day, but it was not a Christmas gift I wanted when I got a call at six in the morning to report to the airport within two hours. Especially after I rushed off to O'Hare to find the flight five hours delayed due to weather, which was followed by another hour-and-a-half of sitting on the tarmac with a plane full of frustrated passengers. The originally scheduled eighteen-hour layover had dwindled all the way down to twelve and it was dark by the time we got there. My room at the same resort hotel was smaller than before and it didn't even have a balcony.

Despite everyone's exhaustion, the captain took the entire crew out for a holiday dinner at a nearby restaurant. There wasn't even enough time for us to drink away our sorrows, so we settled on tacos and good conversation.[4] We talked about the food, our families, our travels, and what we wished we were doing for the holiday. After dinner, we walked back to the hotel, taking the long way back so we could wander around on the dark beach before catching a few hours of sleep in preparation for our early-morning departure.

Christmas in Cancun was my first holiday as a flight attendant away from family or friends. And like many working-holidays afterward, a cool crew making the most out of a less than-ideal situation is what made for a memorably good layover.

Of the hundreds of flights and layovers, I rarely recall the details of most unless they were memorably good or memorably bad. Especially as a reserve flight attendant with little-to-no control over my schedule, I learned to cherish the memorably good ones. I quickly realized that for every really good layover, there was usually a trip (or a series of trips) from hell waiting around the corner. But, during my two and a half years as a reserve and despite a bunch of shitty trips involving long delays, short layovers, crappy airport hotels, and redeyes, I was still fortunate to get quite a few trips with long layovers and I made the most of them as often as I could.

One of the best parts of my new job were layovers in cities where family and friends lived. On a layover in Detroit, I went out to an Italian dinner with my dad. With a sit time in Atlanta, I had a quick lunch with my mother. In downtown San Diego, I met up with my uncle during his lunch break. We went to get shrimp tacos at one of his favorite Mexican restaurants. It had been over ten years since my first cousin Nadeea and I had seen one another. In Seattle, where she lived, she came to visit me at my layover hotel and we talked for hours, catching each other

---

4   By law, flight attendants have to stop drinking alcohol at least eight hours before working a flight.

up on the many missed years of our lives. On one my several trips to Los Angeles, I reconnected with a college friend who had recently moved out there to pursue an acting career. We dined at a swanky Santa Monica restaurant after she gave me a tour of the breathtaking views in Cape Verde. My first visit to Hawaii was on a layover where I hiked Diamondhead with my younger cousin Simone who lived there.

When my family and friends weren't in a layover city, hanging out with the crew could be fun sometimes. However, most of the time, everyone just wanted to hang out at a bar and get drunk, which wasn't really my thing. That quickly got old. I preferred finding something new to see or different to do. It was always great to have one or two fellow crewmembers who shared my desire to explore and were game for venturing out. These were the kind of people, of all ages and from all walks of life, who became my friends, sometimes just for the duration of a trip and often for longer.

When two or three of us decided to go out once we landed, each of us fiercely resisted the urge to retreat to our rooms by making a pact to quickly change and meet back in the lobby. We'd then navigate by an Uber or public transit to shopping districts or attractions recommended by previous crews. Often, our excursions were loosely planned on the plane en route to wherever it was that we were going.

Sometimes though, some crewmembers who already knew what they wanted to do invited others to tag along. My first and second layovers in New York City were memorable thanks to tagging along. On a Saturday spring afternoon, it was Lin, a twenty-something Chinese American who led Grace and I through Chinatown. All of us were new-hire flight attendants and reeled from excitement at scoring such a rare Saturday-in-New-York trip. We strolled through chaotic streets, in and out of shops, playing with souvenirs before eating at a Chinese cafeteria

Lin knew about. Next, we headed over to Brooklyn to wander around and stumbled onto a block party. We grabbed ice-cream before heading back to our uptown hotel to nap before our red eye flight back to Chicago.

Several months later, I worked a flight back to New York City on a Friday with Allen. A few years my senior in terms of employment years, he frequently visited New York and invited me to join him on his bi-weekly empanada run to Empanada Mama in Hell's Kitchen. After empanadas, we met up with Allen's friends at a nearby gay club, where we danced all night. Sober but sleepy, we made it to our morning flight on time.

In Orange County, California, Lewis, Victoria (two senior flight attendants and close friends), and I rented a car. The three of us trekked out to Newport Beach Vineyards for a wine tasting. Late that evening, we met up with Victoria's son in Los Alamitos and at a popular seafood restaurant.

In Anchorage, Lisa and I rented a car and rode along, oohing and aahhing at snowcapped mountains and glaciers that, until then, we'd only seen on TV and in encyclopedias.

Although not a bar person, I hung out with the entire crew at real Irish pubs during my first layover in Ireland. I don't drink beer, but I had a famous Guinness. Everyone loved it. To me, it tasted like dark soapy water.

Hanging out in jazz lounges with the crew in New Orleans and dance clubs in Dallas made up for the long workdays with little sleep. Despite driving me nuts by taking pictures with a selfie-stick along the Baltimore Harbor, Yvonne, a new hire, researched the best crab cakes in Baltimore before we arrived. Waiting in the longest line ever on a hot summer day in St. Louis to try the soul food at Sweetie Pie's was Tasha's ideal. The food was just okay, but we took a picture in front of the sign as proof we were there at the restaurant made famous as a BET television show.

Vince and Sean, two young gay flight attendants who quickly became my in-flight BFFs, ignored my protests to partying after they learned that it was my first Vegas layover. They informed me that getting drunk and gambling was mandatory. Although drinks were free, Vince spent his winnings from a previous trip buying doubles for all of us. Once again, even though I was were exhausted the next afternoon when we headed to the airport to work our next flight, it had been worth it.

While it sometimes lacked sleep, my life was full of fun excursions and fond memories.

STANDING BY AND
SOMETIMES RUNNING

The fact that I could fly for damn-near free in my spare time to almost anywhere in the world didn't sink in for me until a few months after I was hired. And even then, I still wasn't sure how the whole thing worked. Flying standby, also known as "non-revving[5]," as a new-hire reserve during the probationary period was strongly discouraged because not getting back in time and being unavailable for assignment could mean an early end to one's flight attendant career.

"We can travel standby on other airlines too?" I remember skeptically asking another more savvy reserve during one of our work flights. Still learning how to check and list for open

---

5   The term comes from the airlines designation of being a non-revenue
     generating passenger meaning that any costs associated with the booking is
     for required taxes and other government mandated fees. The company does
     not receive any money for the ticket also known as a listing.

seats on the company's intranet system, I was even less familiar with the concept of interline travel where we could apparently fly at low to no cost on other airline carriers as well. Although outlined on the company website, it was still very foreign and confusing. By talking to more experienced flight attendants, I eventually learned how it all worked — or at least, I thought I did.

I started non-revving by going back and forth to Atlanta with more confidence and frequency during my days off. It was usually to grab more stuff that was stored at my mother's house and visit friends for a day or two. I had not yet made the full transition to Chicago. Although I no longer had a home of my own, my car was still in Atlanta too. Once I started non-revving, I enjoyed the quasi-nomadic lifestyle of living in two places. Until I got comfortable with checking available seats and listing on flights, I was super cautious. I always listed myself with more than enough time (at least two days) to get back in case the flights were full, which they usually weren't. If it was a busy day at the airport, I knew that to get the first flight of the day I would need to leave for the airport early in the morning. As my confidence grew, I'd depart a day before I was to report to work with two or three backup flights in mind.

But when the unexpected happened, all bets were off. The dream of flying standby quickly turned into a nightmare. It was a spring day in May when I made a fatal mistake of not checking the weather in advance. Otherwise I would have known thunderstorms were expected throughout the day which meant weather delays and oversold flights.

At 5 a.m., after arriving to Hartsfield Airport for a 6 a.m. flight, I stood in shock, staring at the departure board. The first flight to O'Hare was canceled. I headed to the gate to discover the next flight to Midway airport was oversold. The third oversold flight would also leave without me. I was panicking when my fourth and final flight of the afternoon was indefinitely delayed and filling up quickly. My name was falling to the bottom of a long standby list.

I sat at the gate, uncertain what to do next. It was now evening, and I had been at the airport all day. I frantically texted Anna.

"Try Flight 563 on {*airlines we don't work for*}. The flight leaves in an hour and there are open seats," she replied. "Go to the gate and ask them to list you as a commuter and show them your crew badge."

I had no idea how my airline fairy godmother knew and I didn't care. I simply grabbed my wheeled luggage and hustled over to the terminal on the other side of the airport.

I arrived at the gate, sweaty from walking fast. I waited nervously in line to speak with the agent, wondering if I should allow paying passengers to go in front of me. As a non-rev customer, paying customers were first priority and it was important not to be a nuisance to the gate agents.

"Um, may I list for this flight?" I asked, holding up my crew badge for inspection at the counter. She nodded and began typing away on the computer. I stood silently, convinced she could hear my heart pounding. Could she see that I was scheduled to be back on duty in just a few hours? Would she alert my airlines? How much would this listing set me back? I mean, I know we could fly for a discounted rate, but could I afford however much it was?

"There's five seats and you're number four right now," she said as she handed me a slip without a seat number. "Just hang tight."

I stood off to the side and waited. I kept refreshing the app on my phone to see if there were any updates to my company's delayed flight on the other side of the airport, should I need to bolt.

I watched as boarding for the flight began, longing to be one of the ticketed passengers leisurely strolling through the boarding door. As the last passenger boarded, the agent began calling standby passengers one by one. A small group of six hovered around the boarding door, also anxiously waiting. I stood still, like a statue, with a sweaty grip on my luggage.

"Davis." She called my last name. I raced up to the boarding podium then slowed down, trying to appear calm rather than terrified that, at any moment, a paying customer would materialize behind me to snatch my seat.

I nervously proceeded through the boarding door and went down the jet bridge. I sat in my middle seat and watched the plane's door for the missing passenger whose seat I was taking. I was aware of the stories of standby passengers boarding and then the paying passenger showing up at the last second. The standby passenger and their carry-on luggage would be quickly booted out of the seat. I wasn't safe until the boarding door was closed and we pushed back from the gate.

I was flooded with relief when the flight attendant announced that the boarding door was closed.

"I made it!" I texted Anna, excited from my middle seat when I heard the door close. I landed in Chicago around 10 p.m., two hours before I would go on duty.

"Girl, you cut it close. Be careful - especially on probation. You never know," she replied.

I guess I didn't learn my lesson since several months later, I found myself stuck in Atlanta again. This time, I was on my own. I knew I should have left earlier or at least checked the weather. I had grown tired of getting up and heading to the airport at 3 a.m. on my off days when I always saw plenty of available seats, on later flights. Spending hours running around from gate to gate, watching flights leave without me was the consequence of getting too comfortable.

With no time to sulk or panic, I studied the departures board carefully and prayed to the non-rev gods to show me the way home because directly from Atlanta to Chicago wasn't it.

I approached the customer service for another discount airline that I don't work for.

"I'm trying to get to Chicago, or anywhere near there," I told the agent. I rattled off my employee number and code for my airlines. She listed me on a Milwaukee flight departing in twenty minutes. I thanked her profusely before rushing off to the gate. The last passenger was boarding as I approached the gate agent.

"Hi, I'm listed for this flight." I flashed my badge with confidence as if I was on official company business. She quickly handed me my boarding pass as she closed the door leading down to the plane, indicating boarding was finished.

It was the first time ever flying this particular carrier. As we reached cruising altitude, I exhaled in my cramped aisle seat and pressed along the armrest for the recline button. "Hmm, maybe this plane has a lever instead." There wasn't a lever. I looked over to see that all the seats were upright. "Oh well, I'll just get a drink," I thought as I unlatched my tray table to discover it was half the size of a tray table of most airlines that I'd flown. I watched as I saw the flight attendant was collecting money for soft drinks and bottled waters. At that point, I was certain that this carrier probably doesn't have Wi-Fi either. Despite the lack of amenities, the little discount carrier came through for the day. I was getting closer to Chicago than I was a few hours ago.

Two hours later, we touched down in Milwaukee. As I headed to the car rental place to drive the rest of the way, I passed a gate for a Chicago flight departing in fifteen minutes. I showed the agent my badge and asked her if there was still time to list. She handed me a boarding pass. The flight was wide open.

Wow, I guess no one really comes and goes to Milwaukee.

◆◆◈◆◆

I just knew my standby luck would eventually run out. It had been easy to get to Portland for a travel summit that I'd always wanted to attend; the flights were wide open. But getting back was another story. I wasn't too concerned when I arrived at the airport to find the returning flights were full. I had a few days before I was scheduled to be back on duty. But, I still wasn't thrilled about spending the entire night in the airport. I'd never slept in an airport terminal overnight especially an airport without a crew lounge[6]. But with my funds low from my trip, a few hours in an airport chair wouldn't be too bad.

I began mentally preparing to spend the night in an airport as I watched the boarding door of the last flight leaving from Portland to Chicago close. Every seat of the Alaska Airlines flight was occupied, and it was also the last flight going from the West Coast back east for the day. I was halfway across the small airport, looking for a quiet corner to tuck into for the night, when an unrecognized number popped up on my phone.

"Are you still nearby? There's an open – "

"Yes, I'm coming!" I ran as fast as I could and stayed on the phone with the agent.

"I'm almost there," I kept repeating and huffing into the phone. I approached the gate to find the boarding door open and the agent waving me to hurry through and find row 32. I didn't know and didn't care why the Alaska Airlines flight that had pushed back from the gate had returned.

---

6   Crew lounges for flight attendants are not located at all airports. They are only found at the major hubs of the airlines that a flight attendant works for. You won't find flight attendants for different airlines in the same airport crew lounge.

Once settled in my middle seat, I gave thanks again to God and the gate agent angel. I never had a gate agent ask me for my cell phone when listing for a flight until then. But, when flying standby, I knew not to ask questions nor make requests.

You simply list, wait, and pray you get on.

After I learned the ropes of non-revving, the only thing more exciting was being able to share my access to travel with my friends. One of the perks of my job was buddy passes, which would allow my family and friends to join me on my travels for a discounted rate. But, I quickly found out that most of my friends didn't have the schedule or flexibility to travel standby. Those that did, didn't have the extra money to travel despite the discounted airfare.

Others on my short list of friends were married with kids and didn't have a flexible schedule nor desire to travel standby. There was too much uncertainty. Plus, budget travel really wasn't their thing. Those who had the money worked so that they could afford plane tickets and expensive hotels. They enjoyed staying on resorts and overpaying for package tours. Vacation was a once, maybe twice-a-year thing. Even my platonic guy friend who I designated as my primary travel companion couldn't even travel much because of his job. Once in a while, he used his flight privileges to go from Jersey to Atlanta, but we never got a chance to travel together.

The only person who was occasionally able to travel on a moment's notice was Maya. She was one of my closest friends, still single, and I often thought of her as a little sister, although she was barely a year younger than me. Maya and I met in college when she was a freshman and I was a sophomore in the same dorm. She had flawless ebony skin and a vivacious personality. Her infectious joy often pulled me out of my studious and often too-serious mood. At school, I was known as Nichole, my family called me Nikki, and Maya was the only person who called me KiKi. On campus, she'd greet me with a "Heeeey Ki-Ki!" along with a biggest grin I couldn't help but return. We had a lot in common too. We were both liberal arts students and from the same hometown, although we had gone to different high schools. Maya and I studied, partied, and even pledged the same sorority together.

Had it not been for Maya, I would have spent my college years studying and constantly contemplating how to take over the world. Although she was my little sis, Maya taught me how to have balance in life and laugh, no matter what. Whether we were studying, partying, or just walking across campus back to our dorm, when I was with Maya, I couldn't help but have fun.

When I told Maya that my brother Craig got a temporary work assignment that included corporate housing on a ski resort in the Poconos, she was instantly game for learning how to ski. With so much effort to move to Chicago, I knew it was a while before I transferred to another base. Skiing would be a way for me to try something new and perhaps find something that I could enjoy about winter. Although I could find places to ski in and around Chicago, going to the Poconos to crash with Craig was as good an excuse as any to get on a plane. A travel adventure to experience something new with one of my closest and oldest friends, who finally had the time and budget to travel was something I couldn't pass up. "We got a free place to stay and you can use my buddy passes!" I told Maya.

"It is on! Let's do this KiKi!"

I listed Maya on a flight from Detroit to Jersey and walked her through the entire process of what to do when she arrived at the gate. She easily made it on the flight. Bundled up in our new ski gear, we giggled and screamed with excitement as we met up in the Newark terminal. It was our first girls' trip in years. From the airport, we rented a car and drove to the Camelback Ski Resort in the Poconos. We brought my brother a bottle of Hennessy, his favorite drink, as payment for our three-day stay with him. While he worked all day, Maya and I headed to the ski lodge.

At the lodge, neither Maya nor I paid much mind to the fact that we were the only two Black faces milling about – we were used to being the "only one" in social and professional settings. We ignored the curious glances from kids and other adults as we stood at the counter to purchase our lift tickets, classes, and equipment rental.

"I see why more of our folks aren't out here skiing," Maya said under her breath where only I could hear.

"I know, right! Girl, this is expensive!" I whispered back, emphasizing to Maya with widened eyes.

"We about to ski up and down every mountain to get our money's worth."

Despite paying two hundred dollars each for a first-timer's ski package, neither of us was deterred from our mission of having a good time on the slopes. After getting fitted for boots and skis, we headed to the designated spot for the beginner's class. Still squealing with excitement fueled by crisp air that smelled like freshly washed linen, we marveled at the skiers gliding gracefully down shocking white mounds of snow in the distance. It was a clear, cold, sunny morning. The silent magnificence of the majestic Appalachian Mountains surrounding us held the promise of an amazing day ahead.

It only took Maya one lesson and a half-day of practice before she learned how to ski. Unafraid, she laughed hysterically every time she fell down before quickly hopping right back up.

I, on the other hand, scared of going too fast and falling down, spent the entire day repeatedly gliding, tumbling down, and then flailing around in the snow. It was harder than I thought to get back up with two long slats attached to my feet. Standing up, the ski instructor's directive to place my legs parallel like french fries and bring them together like a pizza to slow down or speed up didn't work for me.

"Yaaaaaaay! I got the haaang of it!" Maya yelled, whizzing by down the bunny hill, successfully maneuvering around me as I sat in the snow, looking for where my ski poles had landed. After I found them, and after a few more attempts, I traded in my ski equipment for a snowboard. I figured if I only had one piece of equipment to worry about, it would be easier to get up and go. Plus, the snowboarders who were twisting and winding their hips down the hills in the distance just looked so much cooler. For the remaining two days, as Maya swished and swooshed down the slopes, I kept tumbling down the bunny slope with equal amounts of determination and frustration. I watched as toddlers effortlessly sped past me repeatedly.

We stayed on the slopes all day and into the evening. Maya often returned to the bunny slopes after a run or two down larger sloaps to check on me. On our second trip to the lodge for lunch and more drinks, Maya shared with me her initial frustrations as well and her excitement when she finally got the hang of skiing.

"No worries Kiki, you'll get it."

"Yeah, and I'm going to have fun trying in the meantime."

"I know what you need – some liquid courage!"

Maya leapt up from the table and went up to the bar, shortly returning with two mugs filled with a warm drink of cinnamon, chocolate, and an indistinguishable liquor.

"Okay, this is a signature drink the bartender made just for us! It's Kahlua, hot cocoa, and vodka – I call it the Camelback Comeback! Here's to never giving up!"

"To never giving up!"

"Or die trying!" we said in unison with raised mugs before bursting into laughter.

At last call for trail runs, Maya talked me into getting off the bunny slope and going with her on the lift to the beginner's hill. With two mugs of Camelback Comeback in my system, the idea seemed didn't seem the least bit frightening until we were on the lift preparing to dismount.

After face-planting off the lift, Maya helped me up and I slowly wiggled to the edge of the incline. It was early into the night. We were the only ones on the hill and my fear of hitting anyone on the way down lessened. Before me was a calm sheet of snow illuminated by flood lights. "Ready KiKi? You got this."

"Ready!"

Maya raced down the hill and I trailed behind. Slowly lifting the edge of my board to pick up speed. I swerved all over the place, unable to figure out how to control the direction of the board. I soon realized despite the lack of control, I was still standing and speeding downhill.

I got this! I screamed to myself. Two seconds later I tumbled down. *Okay, maybe not.* I repeated falling and getting back up all the way down the hill to where Maya waited.

"I saw you staying up! You were doing it!"

I laughed – I was kind of snowboarding. With our unforgettable ski trip adventure coming to an end, we turned and looked up one last time at the deserted incline and the shadow of evergreen trees again a navy night sky. Both of us proud of how far we had progressed in the day and in our lives.

Maya and I turned in our equipment and headed back to my brother's place. The three of us sat around in front of the fireplace while Maya and I recapped the excitement of our days to Craig. We all drank Hennessy, talked, and laughed. Although I was still on my butt more than I was on my feet for most of the time, I was getting the hang of it. I vowed to myself that I would learn how to snowboard better next winter.

It was another surreal moment: in the Poconos at a cabin on a ski resort, having an incredible adventure this time with my dear friend and quality time with my brother. Since starting the job as a flight attendant, despite a constant biting cold, it seemed that quite often my heart was overflowing with warmth. Winter, although still not my favorite season, wasn't so bad after all.

INTERNATIONAL JET-SETTING

The more I traveled, the more my desire for adventure and new experiences grew. Despite the financial limitations and schedule demands, I was determined to take full advantage of the travel opportunities that working as a flight attendant offered. Still, in the first two years, the work was more time-consuming than I had envisioned. I had yet to find the perfect balance between travel for work and travel for leisure, but I was confident I would figure it out. Working as a flight attendant was a better path to the location independence that I had always dreamed about.

Overall, despite the failures with my consulting business, I was finally bouncing back and now progressing once again at a slower, yet steadier, pace. Most importantly, my confidence returned. I felt like a newer but improved version of my old self. My resolve strengthened and my ambition rekindled with each new travel and work challenge I navigated on my own or with the help of others. I was winning again. My gratitude and joy for life shined brighter.

Feeling settled into Chicago while traveling all over the United States, I was ready to take on the world in a new way. Having mastered domestic non-revving, I was often eager to venture further outside my comfort zone. For me, the obvious next step was to start traveling again internationally. This time, it would be on my own time, using my deeply discounted flight benefits and simply for the sake of fun.

The dream of being an international jetsetter, visiting family and friends all over the globe, was alive again. But in reality, Shona was the only person that I knew overseas and kept in touch with. I would officially kick off my personal world tour with a visit to the United Kingdom where she lived!

During my time at Marsha and Miguel's home, Shona and I became good friends. My Chicago family consisted of Marsha, my Jewish mom; Miguel, my Mexican dad; and Shona, my British cousin. A soon-to-be college grad, Shona was studying Mexican-American culture in Chicago as an exchange student, and her parents were family friends of Marsha and Miguel. Thoughtful, sincere, and good-hearted like Marsha and Miguel (who we affectionately called "M&M"), Shona and I had long conversations not just about zombies but also about our tragic romances with men and just navigating life in general. She had arrived in Chicago a few months before I arrived, and thanks to Mike as our wonderful tour guide, we had a chance to explore Chicago's nightlife together from time to time.

I also picked the United Kingdom because it was a bit familiar too. I had visited London for a few days on the way to South Africa fifteen years ago during college, and again for a couple days on the way back. London held fond memories for me as the first time my older brother and I met up in another country. A consultant for Arthur Andersen, Craig had been traveling in Europe for work and was based in London at the time of my travels. From a small town in Michigan, both of us were giddy with excitement and disbelief that as adults we were spending time together in another country.

While in London, I also met my college sweetheart, Elijah. We met in a record store one morning and he then graciously toured me around London during the days while Craig was at work. We kept in touch by email during my time in Africa and Elijah was the reason I passed through London for a few days on the way back. Elijah was my first long-distance relationship and we lasted for over a year with him visiting me twice from London.

Just as Shona was my British cousin, her parents became my cool British aunt and uncle. A recent college grad by the time I visited, Shona lived with her parents in Brighton, two hours outside of London. Ellie (my flight attendant co-worker and friend) and I stayed with them during our visit. Like Marsha and Miguel, they welcomed us like family, and we all had fun getting to know one another. Thanks to John and Julie, Ellie and I got the full British host-family experience. We giggled as we happily accepted offers of tea with milk each morning and evening. We delighted in their accents and discovered the awesomeness of rubber hot water bottles that they gave us each night to keep our feet warm in bed. Ellie and I couldn't decide if Shona's dad, a college professor, looked more like the British actor Hugh Grant or the British actor Colin Firth. Both she and I would laugh at John's corny dad jokes while Shona would roll her eyes in mock annoyance. We fell in love with Shona's mom, Julie, who was the perfect combination of hip and zany, with dyed bright red hair cut in a stylish bob that matched her personality. "You have the coolest parents ever!" we told Shona on several occasions. Kidding around constantly and teasing one another, her parents were easy-going, fun-loving, and goofy. They shared with us the best places to go in and around Brighton and in London. A few nights before we left, John cooked a big dinner in honor of our visit. Afterwards, we all gathered in the living room to listen to music and enjoy evening tea. With my new camera, we took silly candid pictures of one another to take back and share with Marsha and Miguel.

Despite the chilly November days, Shona toured Ellie and I through the shops and cafes in The Lanes, a popular shopping district in Brighton. We marveled at the grand interior of the famous Royal Pavilion, which was the former seaside retreat turned museum of British princes and kings. We posed for pictures along the water at the Brighton Palace Pier as if it were summer rather than a rainy fall evening. To take a break from the cold, we ducked into dark pubs for beers and quaint cafes for sandwiches and more tea. We spent the final two days of our five-day "holiday"[7] in London during the day and going to clubs at night.

Ellie and I ended our epic overseas adventure in business-class from Heathrow back to O'Hare. Still giddy with excitement from all our new experiences, we sipped champagne, programmed our movies to start at the same time, and made sure to take full advantage of the lie-flat seats. We wished for more time to eat, sleep, and watch movies as our flight came to an end and our reserve days began again.

Although I've had some good vacations, I wasn't sure if there would ever be another international trip as memorable as our time in the United Kingdom. But little did I realize that it

---

7   The British term for vacation.

was just the beginning of a series of unforgettable adventures with friends both old and new.

A COSTA RICAN ROAD TRIP

L ondon was really a baby step outside my comfort zone. Especially since I'd been there before and already knew people who lived there. It gave me a chance to learn the ropes of international non-revving and go someplace relatively safe, should I get stranded.

Costa Rica, my second international leisure trip as a flight attendant, was a different story. I didn't know anyone who lived in Costa Rica and had never been there before, but it was always someplace I'd wanted to go. Plus going to Costa Rica would give me a chance to put my six years of high school and college Spanish classes to use. My travel buddy this time was another coworker, Dana. She and I quickly became friends on the jumpseat[8] during a two-day work trip. Both single, from the same hometown, we talked about our need to be more adventurous. Costa Rica was

---

8   A fold down seat, often located in front, back and exit doors of an airplane where flight attendants must sit during takeoff and landing.

on both of our travel bucket lists, so we decided together would non-rev there together on our next days off.

Adding to our goal to be more daring, we were going to just wing it too – Thelma and Louise style. Our rough plan included renting an inexpensive car and road-tripping through the country. We'd find cheap hotels and hostels to stay at along the way. With a little bit more travel experience and decent Spanish, I wasn't as nervous as Dana, who surprisingly hadn't done much international traveling although she'd worked a few more years than I had as a flight attendant. After researching the loads (unsold seats on flights), we met up at the airport and flew into the Liberia International Airport in Costa Rica.

The first hiccup we encountered was at the rental car counter. The day rate we booked online was affordable, as our research showed, but the insurance tripled our costs. We bought the cheapest plan for a one-week rental, which left us on the hook for a charge of at least $3,000 should the car be damaged. Discouraged that the trip had the potential to be not as cheap as we hoped, we considered declining the car and just heading back home. But we didn't.

Instead, we rented the car and drove carefully away. For the most part, the highways looked like any other city with heavy traffic, but the signs were in Spanish. It was our first time driving in another country. About two hours into our drive, as we moved farther away and higher up into mountains, the wide, multi-lane paved roads narrowed and turned to gravel. We cautiously maneuvered the Toyota Corolla around crater-sized potholes on the crushed stone roads and braced for a jerk or jolt when they were impossible to avoid. We bounced up and down in our seats listening to rocks crunching underneath the tires and pebbles pinging the undercarriage of the vehicle. We envied the Jeeps, trucks, and motorbikes zipping past us at the normal speed limit as we bumped along. We both glued our eyes to the road no matter who was driving. Every hour, we took turns driving while the other prayed out loud for the car not to get damaged. Despite our research on road-tripping in Costa Rica, none of the online experts had informed of us the absolute need for a vehicle with four-wheel-drive capabilities.

"Dear Heavenly Father, Lord Almighty, we ask that you keep us safe on this journey," said Dana.

"Yes, Father God." I replied with equal fervor and reverence.

"We ask that you keep this car safe, protected, and free from harm."

"Yes, Lord puh-lease."

"We ask for your help because, you know, our finances, and we cannot afford to pay any fines for damage. We ask for your favor, your grace, and mercy. We know that in your name all things our possible."

"*All* things are possible, including navigating this road."

"In Jesus' name, we pray. Amen."

"Amen."

Our two-hour drive to our first stop, Tamarindo Bay, turned into four because we were driving so slowly. It was late afternoon when we arrived. The crunchy gravel road of Route 152 gradually transformed into smooth pavement once again as we entered the beachside town lined with small shops, boutique hotels, and restaurants. Surfers and sunbathers sauntered around in swimsuits. For two battle-weary drivers who had observed the idyllic scene from the car, we felt as if we had reached our paradise destination as the ocean breeze cleared the road dust from our nostrils. After parking, we walked around to the boutique hotels lined up along the strip between the shops, inquiring about available rooms and prices. After a few inquiries and before sunset, we found a nice, inexpensive beachfront bungalow situated directly on the beach. We paid twenty five dollars apiece for the two-bedroom ocean-view room. This was the budget luxury we were hoping for! We celebrated surviving our first day and our gem of a hotel by lounging on the sandy white beach, drinking wine as the sun set.

Forging ahead the next morning along Route 145 to our next destination, we were well rested and relaxed as we drove a couple of hours along paved roads once again. Although it was the dry season in Costa Rica, we enjoyed the sprawling greenish-brown fields and palm trees lining the highway. After a few hours, we stopped for snacks at a small countryside convenience market. We chatted it up with the owner, Eduardo, who shared with us the best places to visit in Costa Rica. We learned about his family, his friends, and the most popular foods to try in the country (which included his churros). We each devoured several of the sugary fried dough sticks that neither of us had ever eaten before. After a lengthy and engaging conversation with Eduardo, we stocked up on more of his churros to snack on, and hit the road again on our way to Monteverde.

Located in Central Costa Rica, this village is known for its famous cloud forest located 1,500 meters above sea level. Described as a lush tropical rainforest high above the clouds, it was a "must see" destination for nature lovers. As the elevation began to increase, the roadways once again narrowed and turned to gravel. We kept driving, praying, and going around the potholes along a nonstop winding road that just kept getting narrower, steeper, and more rugged with each passing mile. Along with hitting a pothole, we were now worried about falling off the edge of the road. With the sun setting and the roads getting scarier, we breathed a sigh of relief when we reached the small village right before nightfall. We had no idea if we were even near the cloud forest and we didn't care. We just wanted to get off the road.

The weather had drastically changed during our drive; as the sun set, the temperature dropped. The night air was chilly with a slight mist. It had gone from a hot summer day to a crisp fall night in less than a few hours. Dana and I checked into the first budget hotel we could find. It was a small, dank, musty room with two tiny twin beds above a small souvenir shop. With a fluorescent bulb in the ceiling as the only source of light, it was nowhere near as nice as our beach bungalow. But we were too tired and hungry to look around for another place.

After dinner at the adjacent restaurant that was as unimpressive as our hotel room, we walked around the small town that seemed home to more young backpackers than locals. Our waitress mentioned something about a night festival nearby that she recommended we check out. It was still early on a Saturday night, and although tired from driving, we remembered our vow for adventure. After assurance that the festival was nearby, we reluctantly drove father into town along a flat, dark road and parked among the crowd of cars lining the road. We walked for a few minutes into a dark grassy field following the silhouettes of locals heading in the same direction. Around a bend of trees where everyone was headed came a flood of colored lights. We were in the right place.

Festive salsa and merengue instantly hit our ears. To our surprise and delight, we had stumbled upon a massive Costa Rican carnival. Strings of lights lined endless rows of booths with local vendors selling handicrafts, toys, and every food imaginable. There were roasted pigs, barbecued chicken drumsticks, grilled sausages, roasted corn, and of course more churros. On the other side of the large field were carnival rides and games for children. We joined the families, kids, and teens wandering about the fairgrounds. Amazed at all that was happening around us, we kept walking, following the direction of the crowd that was headed into a small wooden arena at the end of all the stalls. Without any idea what was inside, we paid our entry fee into what we discovered was a bullfight.

We followed the crowd to go underneath the bleachers in order to get a view of the show. It was our first bullfight and neither of us could believe we were so close to the arena floor, separated from the bull by only a wooden fence. We screamed as the massive, horned beast writhed and bucked with agitation while the crowd and several matadors taunted him. The bull angrily circled the large arena and peered right into the wooden fence where we stood. We squealed again with fear and excitement as the crowd cheered. On several occasions, bold and foolish men sitting atop of the fence jumped into the ring to get the bull's attention. They ran and jumped back over the fence as soon as the bull began to charge. During the intermission between the fights, we watched as Costa Rican cowboys ran alongside and attempted to mount running horses. Some were more successful than others. All the while, an announcer shouted over the stadium megaphone in rapid-fire Spanish that neither of us understood. Energized after a long journey, we could not believe our good fortune once again.

It wasn't until the next morning that Dana and I realized that we were actually in the Costa Rican rainforest. When we had arrived the previous day after dark, we hadn't been able to see how lush or how green the trees were. Surrounding the small village was vibrant green foliage and a dense, misty fog, as if we had stepped into an entirely different ecosystem from the dusty, daytime highway roads we had traveled. If we weren't already in it, we knew the famous Cloud Forest was nearby as we left the village and drove even higher up the mountain to the Monteverde Nature Preserve for a zip line tour.

Dana had never ziplined, and it had been over a decade since I tried it at an obstacle course park in Atlanta. I expected something similar that would allow us to climb and play in the trees. As usual, we were excited and nervous.

"You can add the Tarzan swing and Superman tour for seven more dollars!" said the cashier in perfect English.

We didn't know exactly what that was, but we looked at each other and nodded.

"Do you all want the picture package for $49.99?" asked the cashier.

Already over our budget for the ziplining tour, we looked at each other again.

"What do you think?" I asked Dana skeptically. I figured we could just take pictures of each other swinging along the zip lines.

"Well, how many times are we going to be zip lining in the rainforest?"

I nodded. We agreed to split the picture package, bringing our ziplining tour up to seventy US dollars each. We sighed as we each handed the clerk our credit cards.

With harness and helmets fastened, we joined a group of five other guests and two tour guides in a clearing of the dark forest. A tall steel platform connected by a small zip line was set up. Our tour guides, two young Costa Rican men, casually climbed up the platform and gave us a quick demonstration of how to attach our harnesses to the line. We could tell it was a demo they had given many times before. We then hiked further along, Dana and me lagging behind, admiring the massive trees stretched for what seemed like miles into the air. Chirps, buzzing, and the soft crunching of wet leaves and moss beneath our feet was oddly relaxing. In every direction were vivid shades of green ferns, plants, and shrubs among black earth and tree trunks. Ten minutes later, we reached another metal platform not much higher than the first. One by one, we carefully climbed the thin metal ladder to an opening in the sky among the thick layers of leaves.

At the top, we gasped. We were high above the forest canopy and overlooking a deep valley of emerald trees that stretched for miles. A thin wire about a mile long stretched across the valley.

This was nothing like my previous zipline experience that had transported me a few feet from tree to tree, but not above an entire forest. Standing on the platform, I could barely see where the wire would end. My heart dropped as the guides quickly connected the others ahead of us and pushed them along the zip line to who knows where. Several of them screamed as their feet launched from the platform. They were twisting and twirling as they hurled forward.

"You can go ahead of me," I told Dana as we stood at the top of the platform. Her eyes wide with fear, she adamantly shook her head. There was nowhere to go; looking down at how high we had just climbed was worse than looking across. The handlebars flew back across the line to us and the guide instructed me to grab them. I gripped the handles for dear life as he quickly hooked the harness on. Before I could fully crouch as instructed in the demo, the guide pushed me forward. My body went spinning in a circle as I moved along the line screaming.

"Aaaahhhhhh!!!!!!"

"Bend your knees!" shouted the instructor.

I bent my knees and the spinning slowed as the speed forward increased. I kept screaming, certain I would fall hundreds of feet, forever lost, into the thick blanket of green leaves. The wind snatched my scream and I looked straight ahead to the approaching platform. The tour guide on the other side pulled me onto the landing as my feet touched down. Moments later, Dana came into view with a look of terror on her face. Shaking, we climbed the short distance towards the second platform. The rest of the group was already a few feet ahead of us on the trail. Dana and I, with our hearts still racing, looked at each other in disbelief and then grinned as we walked along to catch up with the others.

Less terrifying, but equally high, was another line among the canopy tree tops. Prepared for what was to come this time, I quietly enjoyed the view as I zipped across. The feeling of flying was exhilarating. At our next stop in the forest, I was preparing for my Tarzan shout that I practiced in my head as I grabbed the swinging rope. My shout turned into a surprised yelp as the rope I expected to smoothly glide from one platform to the other, plummeted my body down several feet before swaying erratically to the other side. I was laughing by the time it stopped. On my stomach for the final, mile-long Superman line, gusts of wind quickly blew the tears of pure wonder that streamed down my cheeks as I soared face down and arms outstretched through clouds high above the rolling forest hills. I was so grateful to be fully alive to experience such a moment.

Heading back to the car after laughing at our photos, Dana and I reminisced about the experience of a lifetime. We debated about who was more terrified and the audacity of our tour guides politely ignoring our pre-launch hesitation.

We ended our unforgettable trip with a slow car ride back to Liberia that afternoon, stopping at a coffee plantation for a tour and finally one more stop at a beach hotel, where we watched the sunset. In the morning, we took a last-minute snorkeling excursion before heading to the airport for our afternoon flight. Before leaving Monteverde, we popped out a small dent in the car and polished out the small scrapes caused by potholes. We successfully and quickly returned the car without any visible damage.

So many things could have gone wrong for two single women traveling through the mountains of Costa Rica in a Toyota Corolla. But they didn't. Together we had moments of fear, frustration, and a lot of hesitation about what could go awry. Of the many lessons we learned from our adventures in Costa Rica, we realized that reward requires taking risks and pushing beyond our fears. With faith and an optimistic attitude, things always worked out – sometimes even better than we could have imagined. Dana and I landed back in Chicago with memories of an unforgettable adventure that took us outside our comfort zone that had just grown a bit bigger.

COFFEE, TEA, OR ME? PART I

It's Saturday night at Cafe Iberico in downtown Chicago. The crowded restaurant buzzes with chatty diners. The array of authentic Spanish tapas and red wine transports me back to my recent trip to Barcelona. It had been a month since I'd seen George. After a series of tentative plans that had been canceled due to my flying schedule, he and I were finally catching up.

We needed to talk.

I get to the table and George is already there waiting. Although he's trying to hide it, a look of annoyance that I'm late flashes across his handsome face. He's wearing a snug black sweater showing off his exceptionally muscular frame, complementing his smooth copper-brown skin. After ordering seafood paella, braised beef and spicy potatoes along with a bottle of Tempranillo, we dive into serious conversation.

"So, what's going on with you and this guy in Jersey?"

I pause, hesitant to disclose painful details of a short-lived fling. I frown and then follow with a heavy sigh as I slowly shake my head.

George rolls his eyes. "Girl, I knew he wasn't the one for you."

We move on as I confess my other indiscretions one by one.

"I talked to The Asshole the other day," I say, flatly referring to another old flame as our desserts of flan, chocolate bread pudding and arroz con leche arrives. "We had a good conversation catching up, but it's not happening either. Been there. Done that. Got the t-shirt and the souvenir video."

"Oooh, *video*," says George with excited inquisitiveness.

"A metaphor. Simply a metaphor."

George's face drops. He gives me a look of disdain followed by the side-eye of judgment as he sips his espresso.

"You can do better. Now, let's focus on more important matters." He leans in closer, gives me a playfully seductive stare as he gently caresses my hand. "So, when are you and I going away together?"

If it were not for the minor detail that George is gay and does not share my love of internet memes, the two of us would make a good couple. As my self-appointed gay boyfriend-slash-relationship advisor, George has been privy to the most intimate details of my dating life as a single thirty-something woman. I'd been flying for a few years now, and while the flight attendant edition of the dating game had been fun, it had also been frustrating.

Dating is a challenge for anyone. Dating as a flight attendant adds a new layer of challenges, but also different opportunities as well. Travel and adventure are a part of the package with me. And, I like that my dating pool is wider because I'm not limited by geography. While there are some crazy suggestions on the Internet about what men need to know to "land" a flight attendant, there are websites and other flight crew blogs that give some pretty truthful tips about how to be in a relationship with someone who's constantly on the go.

Whatever motivations men or women may have about dating a flight attendant, I have faith that it's still all about finding the right person at the right time. I'm still learning to weed out the scrubs from those who are sincere, genuine, and looking for something serious. They understand the importance of respect, honesty, integrity, and trust between two people.

It's true, my co-workers and I are constantly on the go. That doesn't mean we are flighty (no pun intended) or against commitment. Many of us want and many of us have partners who share our passion for travel and also value family and commitment. Others have mates who don't like to travel, and I, personally, don't understand how they do it. But they do.

So, reflecting on my own adventures and misadventures, I've been throwing the frogs back into the pond as quickly as possible.

I'm also learning how to better navigate the rules of the dating game – the flight attendant edition. In the meantime, George is taking me out to dinner, gets all my buddy passes, and an unlimited supply of pretzel snacks.

Like that Lisa Stansfield song, one of my eighties favorites, "I've been around the world and I can't find my baby."

I feel like that sometimes. I've dated a lot of men from different backgrounds and cultures while searching for "The One." Even before I was a flight attendant and for as long as I can remember, I dated men of different nationalities. I never set out to do so, it just worked out that way.

My first boyfriend ever, when I was sixteen, was Haitian-American. My college boyfriend, who lived in London, was from Zimbabwe. Andre, "the one that got away," was Jamaican. Although not exclusively, I do have a track record of dating "foreigners," as my uncles called several of my suitors. In a good-natured fashion, they often teased me mercilessly about the guys I dated.

"Where's your boyfriend from again?" Uncle Alan would ask. "Zamunda?"

He and my other uncle would then crack up with laughter before imitating African accents and their favorite movie scenes from *Coming to America*. In all fairness, my uncles were equal opportunity when it came to teasing their niece about her boyfriends, no matter their country of origin. Fortunately, it was never when the boyfriend was around, but I was nevertheless utterly mortified while my uncles just enjoyed playing the Dozens.[9]

But truth be told (and despite what my uncles may argue), not all the guys I dated were from other countries. I don't have a type. Actually, some are American born. Most are of the same race as I am. But, as I traveled internationally and domestically, my dating pool inevitably expanded. The result has been unforgettable dates in Chicago and throughout the world with a variety of men. Like my layovers, there have been some memorably good ones and others I wish I could forget. There's even been a few that turned into meaningful relationships, and some which just make for amusing stories.

Paul was the first guy I semi-seriously dated as a flight attendant. It was the start of my first summer travel season with the airlines and I was working red-eye flights back-and-forth from Chicago

---

9   The Dozens is a cultural past time among Black folks that involves comedic trash-talking and unscripted roasting. Usually it's about the other person's mother, but not always.

to LA. On my short layovers in LA, I started jogging at a high school track near the hotel. One afternoon while working out, a well-built, caramel-colored stranger in a Nike t-shirt and shorts kept sprinting around the track as I barely trotted the loop. His endurance motivated me to pick up the pace and do several more laps than intended. Collapsing on the bleachers after my workout, the fit and friendly stranger approached and congratulated me.

"I saw you out there hustlin," he commented, nodding approval.

"I was trying to keep up with you," I replied only halfway joking.

From there, Paul and I struck up a conversation about our workout regimes and agreed to be running partners whenever I was in town again. To my surprise, I was assigned to work flights with LA layovers with more frequency and ended up seeing Paul several times that month. We'd meet up to run around the track where we first met. A couple times, we speed-hiked up the Culver City stairs to the Baldwin Hills overlook.

Most of the time, Paul and I would meet up for a couple of hours to work out before I headed back to the hotel to get ready for an evening flight. Although at times shy, he was easygoing and down-to-earth. I appreciated his passion for fitness. In between my trips, we'd text one another an occasional hello. He was never a big talker and I wasn't crazy about texting, so it worked out. It was just cool to have a workout buddy in LA. Still trying to adjust to the new flight attendant life, I really wasn't interested in dating just yet or having a stereotypical out-of-town flight attendant fling.

That's the reason why I really didn't take Paul seriously when he invited me to come and hang out on one of my days off. Even when he said we could do anything I wanted, I didn't believe him. But, I said parasailing because it was simply the first thing that popped into my mind of things I've always wanted to do.

"Huh?" They have parasailing in LA?"

"I have no idea," I said, laughing at my outrageous suggestion.

A few days later, Paul texted me; he had found a place and wanted to see what day worked for us to go parasailing. *Oh, he wasn't kidding.*

A couple weeks later, he and I were floating in the sky over Venice Beach. Strapped together in a parachute kite, we gently glided higher and higher above the Pacific waters as a speedboat towed us along. We sat next to each other, feet dangling as we admired the panoramic view of a boundless powder-blue sky kissing endless turquoise waters. It was the first parasailing experience for both of us and we were both in awe. Once back in the boat and headed to shore as the sun set, Paul gave me his jacket to keep me warm. Had you looked up "romantic" in the dictionary at that moment, there would have been a picture of me, nestled comfortably in Paul's arms, his oversized bomber jacket wrapped around me, and both of us smiling at each other. After parasailing, we went out to dinner at an upscale burger restaurant in Santa Monica before he dropped me off at the airport in the evening. If there were such a thing, Paul would have won the award for the best date ever.

Throughout the summer, when I was in LA, my time was spent with Paul. He'd pick me up from the hotel and we'd go work out, depending on how much time I had before my evening flight. Sometimes, we would stay in and watch TV. None of our dates were as spectacular as the first, but he had set the bar high.

A few months later, I came to visit Paul again on one of the few weekends I was off. It was the first time I was staying overnight at his place. I'm not sure why, but Paul, a hotel front desk manager, didn't tell me (via text) until after I landed that he had to work over the weekend. He said he'd "be home shortly," and suggested I take an Uber to his place. I sat eating takeout alone in his sparsely furnished bachelor pad. *Why didn't he tell me to come another weekend? This is some bullshit.*

"Shortly" ended up being five hours later. He arrived stressed out and barely apologetic. Neither of us spoke much. That night, when he mentioned he would be working the next day, I moved my evening flight to a morning one. I was scheduled to work on Sunday. In that moment, I realized that, like the uniform dress, trekking out to LA on my few off-days wasn't practical or sustainable.

Paul and I were never officially together so we didn't officially break up. There wasn't a talk. Paul was busy with work and our hangouts on my short layovers were convenient for him, but spending longer amounts of time together on a regular basis was not. It really wasn't for me either, yet we gave it a try that didn't work. In the subsequent weeks, we both simply faded out of each other's lives. Occasionally, but not always, I would text Paul when I was in town. He was frequently working late. Eventually, I stopped texting. His frequent "hellos" were fewer and fewer. I was okay with the memories of a summer fling in LA and an unforgettable first date.

Coming in second as an unforgettable date was the French B-Boy.

My crew, although pleasant to work with, were all more senior than me. I could tell they had little interest in showing the junior flight attendant around on her first visit to Paris. It was like that sometimes. I was going to be on my own unless I happened to meet a handsome French gentleman to show me around town. The made-for-TV fantasy was all worked out in my head. I just needed to find a co-star...

He was the only other dark face among the sea of white passengers boarding my flight from New York to Paris and he was cute too. Out of the corner of my eye as I prepared the cabin for departure, I immediately noticed his smooth, dark chocolate skin, and deep-set eyes. Despite having the swag of a New York b-boy complete with a fitted Yankees cap, shell top Adidas, and Beats headphones around his neck, I knew he was not American. Probably French-African. The ease with which he settled into his coach seat near the back of the plane for the nine-hour flight told me that he was also a frequent international traveler. Working up front for most of the flight, I didn't give much thought to the cute passenger. The few times I passed his row (that he had to himself), I noticed that, like most passengers, he was asleep.

As we got ready to land, he stirred from his sleep and asked for a glass of water as I approached his row collecting trash from the aisle. He spoke with the effortless formality of a person fluent in both French and English. "Sure," I replied, and smiled warmly. His eyes locked with mine for a second longer than necessary.

Everything in the galley was put away, but I didn't mind accommodating. I quickly returned from the galley and gave him another smile as I handed him the cup of water he requested. He thanked me, smiling back and locking eyes again.

When I returned to collect his empty cup, I got up the nerve to talk with him. The crew was finished with our landing duties and just waiting around until it was time to take our seats. It was the perfect time to strike up a conversation and my last chance to either make a new friend or get insider tips on the best things to do solo.

"Are you returning home or visiting Paris?" I not-so-innocently asked. That was the best I could do for a pickup line and I was hoping he would give me a long rather than short answer.

"Yes, I was visiting my family for a few weeks in the States," he said, smiling. "I'm ready to be home though. How long will you be staying here?"

Yas! I got the long answer and a follow-up question.

"Only for twenty-four hours, and then we head back," I said, still smiling and not breaking eye contact.

From there, Frantz and I began chatting for the next few minutes, I casually yet strategically shared with him that it was my first time in Paris and asked for his recommendations on things to do. As the final bell chimed indicating it was time to be seated, Frantz asked me out to dinner. I quickly gave him my number. It only took a bit of effort, and my wish for a handsome tour guide to show me around the city of love was granted.

Later that evening, I met Frantz in my hotel lobby and we took a cab to dinner. During the ride, Frantz shared with me more about his background. Born in Ghana, he and his family had lived in France for most of his life. He had family in New York and they were in the import export business. As I guessed, he frequently traveled to and from the States. As he chatted away, I did my best to listen intently while gazing over his shoulder out the window. It was nighttime and I had no idea where we were going. Although I assumed not far, we drove away from the pristine, tree-lined boulevards of the high-end tourist district.

I hoped my tour guide wasn't a serial killer as we took winding cobbled stone roads through a bustling working-class commercial district. The streets were filled with black and brown faces milling about the sidewalks. We passed block after block of brightly lit cafes, small markets, and fruit stands until arriving at a storefront restaurant serving West African cuisine. We were the only ones in the quaint cafe of five or six small dining tables covered with orange and red kente cloth. Artwork of rural African villages adorned the walls along with an array of wooden tribal masks. The owner, a tall older man with graying hair, greeted us as if Frantz was a close friend and regular VIP diner. Deserted on a busy night, yet open for business, it looked as if the restaurant was closed down just for the two of us. Or at least, that was what I hoped. I pushed aside the alternative that the food sucked.

It was romantic, like something out of a movie. Frantz was the perfect gentleman, ushering me to the table and pulling out my chair. Over a candlelit dinner of spicy fish, Jollof rice, and plantains, our conversation flowed. He listened attentively and we continued flirting with our eyes while we sat across from one another. Enamored with each other as well as the food, the questions eventually turned to our respective relationship statuses.

"Tell me," he said, sipping his glass of wine before leaning slightly back in his chair. "How could someone as beautiful as you be single?"

Though it was a frequent and banal question, but it sounded sincere coming from him. I soaked up the flattery as I chewed slowly to give myself a chance to decide if I would give a genuine answer.

"I'm not sure," I replied, choosing a vague cliché. "I guess I haven't met the right one."

I held my gaze on him before shifting the conversation back his way.

"What about you?"

He sighed as if reflecting on the choices in his life while leaning forward to gather a forkful of rice from his plate, his eyes locking deeply with mine.

"My wife just doesn't understand who I am," he confided as if coming to terms with a hard truth.

I blinked slowly while taking a gulp rather than the intended sip of my wine. I pursed my lips and faked a sympathetic nod. My romantic interest in him evaporated faster than a drop of water on a hot skillet. I focused on chewing and pretended to care about Frantz's tumultuous marriage. I debated my options.

I could storm out, furious about the fact that I unknowingly agreed to go out with a married man. True, I didn't know where I was, but could grab a taxi back to the hotel. Or, I could switch to homie mode and enjoy the rest of the night.

I chose homie mode.

For the rest of the dinner, I returned his seductive gazes with polite yet blank stares to hide my annoyance and disappointment.

After dinner, Frantz offered to show me around Paris at night. It was still early, so I figured, why not? We headed out of the restaurant and walked to the train station heading to the city center. Still wide awake having slept the day away, I was eager to see more of the city and tried not to care about my guide's marital status. Overall, we were still enjoying each other's company as Frantz carried on as if to be married and dating was perfectly normal. I know the French are more liberal than Americans, but not that liberal.

Our first stop was the Louvre Museum. Although closed, lights flood the spacious courtyard of the historic palatial complex. In the center of the courtyard, large glowing glass pyramids shone brilliantly. I was in awe as I recalled the scene from the movie *Inferno* with Tom Hanks. *Oh, so this is where it was filmed!* I had to stop myself from climbing up and running along the glass and metal structure from excitement. Frantz relished my childlike wonder. We took pictures of one another, like corny tourists throughout the courtyard and in front of the pyramids. The surrealness of the experience finally hit me – I was in Paris!

As we strolled along to our next stop, leaving the Louvre behind, I looked up at the Eiffel Tower, sparkling with millions of tiny dancing lights. Although I had seen it earlier during the day from the airport shuttle window, the tall metal spire was now transformed into something magical. On a chilly September night, I fell love with the fabled City of Lights – the one that until that day, I had only seen in magazines and movies.

Locked arm in arm, we slowly wandered to the Avenue de Champs-Élysées, peering through the windows of luxury boutiques. A fashionista, Frantz was engrossed in the store displays and was eager to show me the retail homes of Gucci, Louis Vuitton, and Chanel. Had I been wealthy or a shopaholic, perhaps I would have been more impressed by the world's most famous commercial streets, but it was simply amusing to watch him peer with intense interest at the designer goods. It was getting colder as we made our way to Arc de Triumph, where we took more pictures underneath the towering, illuminated arch. At around eleven that night, we headed back to the hotel, still arm in arm until we reached the lobby.

"Wow, I had such a wonderful time," I told Frantz.

"You are an amazing woman. It was my pleasure. I hope you'll return again to Paris."

"I will."

But not to see you...

I really was getting tired and didn't have to force a yawn, as Frantz continued to walk slowly with me through the lobby to the elevator.

He stared at me intently and lingered. His hands were in his pocket as I pressed the elevator button.

I knew exactly where our night was leading.

I appreciatively smiled at Frantz and thanked him again for such an unforgettable evening. I leaned in slowly and gave him the dreaded church hug.[10] The elevator doors opened I stepped in alone, waved goodbye, watching the disappointment register on his face as the doors closed.

---

10 As defined by the online Urban Dictionary: A hug in which a hugger deliberately maintains distance to avoid pelvic and chest contact. For a male romantically interested in a female, a church hug is equivalent to the kiss of death, signaling zero possibility of sexual intimacy and permanent placement in the friend zone.

◆◆◈◆◆

Speaking of disappointment, passenger 17C who I called "Googly Eyes" was one of those can't-forget moments that I wish I could. As many do, it started off great...

The second time I walked through the cabin to collect trash, the handsome dark-haired guy with wire-rimmed glasses and curly black hair smiled at me sheepishly again as I passed his seat. Back in the galley, I mentioned to my co-workers that I had an in-flight boyfriend who kept giving me googly eyes. By the time we landed, I'd forgotten all about him until he strode to the back of the plane where I was unloading my luggage instead of exiting the aircraft with the last of the passengers on board. He thanked me again before quickly handing me a piece of paper that I knew wasn't trash. Along with his name and number was a note that read:

Your beautiful smile was the highlight
of my long travel day.

Several days later, I called Googly Eyes, whose name was Mitchell. A college professor in West Virginia, Mitchell traveled to Chicago every few months to visit his son who lived with his ex-wife. I've never dated a professor before and after checking out his profile on the university website and stalking him on Facebook, I was further intrigued. His area of expertise was sociology, and he was a published author of several books with an eclectic taste in music that mirrored mine. As I imagined, our conversations were intellectually stimulating as we learned more about one another. There was an instant chemistry over the phone. I liked that Mitchell was analytical and self-aware. He had the maturity of a man who had a master's degree and was going for tenure and a PhD. After a couple of long phone conversations, we were looking forward to seeing each other again.

The next month, Mitchell mentioned that he would be in town and suggested that I pick my favorite restaurant or a new one that I wanted to try. It had been a while since I had been on a date and the neighborhood was full of small, intimate restaurants. I settled on a modest Argentinian restaurant, and we planned to meet there at around 6 p.m. Less than an hour before our date, Mitchell sent an unusually long text that read kinda like a page of a diary:

> Nichole, I'm going to cancel. It's money. I'm sitting here trying to juggle my budget in order to afford a nice meal out, even a modestly priced one, and I'm growing increasingly anxious rather than excited. I was excited about spending some time with you, but after much resistance, denial I suppose, I lack the financial resources and emotional space even for a casual date, let alone anything potentially beyond that. I'm sorry about not being straight with you and jerking you around in the process. I enjoyed getting to know you a little and wish you all the best. goodbye.

In other words Mitchell was either too broke, scared, or both, to go out with me. I was a bit baffled. Although accustomed to canceled dates and no-shows, this one was a Hall of Fame nominee. I was dumped at the last minute, by text, complete with a "Dear Jane" letter, before the first date. During our conversations, he'd never mentioned any financial challenge. I hadn't pegged him for a high-anxiety type of guy. I thought we had talked openly and honestly. We hadn't even talked about our relationship goals or expectations. But somehow, our meeting was overwhelming for him.

I was a bit pissed off. I was really looking forward to seeing Mitchell again. I decided to wait a little while before replying to his text. Internally, after my initial surprise, I was rolling my neck, wagging my fingers, and thinking to myself *"Oh no, he just didn't!"*

But, he just did, and replying in such a state wouldn't be worth the negative energy expended. Instead, after processing my emotions (which moved from surprise, to disappointment, to annoyance, and finally, acceptance), I replied with a much shorter text. I wished Mitchell the best of luck with his life and encouraged him in the future to consider coffee dates or pick up the phone to communicate important matters face-to-face.

His reply:

> Thanks, you're right!

In hindsight, Mitchell hid his emotional immaturity well, unlike Jean Charles. The night we officially met, Jean Charles sat at the bar, drinking a glass of wine when I walked into the Hilton Hotel at O'Hare, dragging my wheeled suitcase behind me with an apologetic look on my face. I was running a few minutes late for our first date. He wore a freshly pressed blue shirt and gray slacks. Thank God – he looked like the picture I saw of him on Match.com, which displayed a handsome man with chocolate skin, magnetic eyes, and a well-manicured beard. He stood up to greet me as I approached. We were both happy to finally meet in person.

"Mind if we sit over here?" I asked, pointing to a table away from the bar.

I was still in uniform and whether on or off-duty, hanging out at the bar is a huge company no-no. Plus, I was technically still on duty. It was a slow night on airport standby and I hadn't gotten an assignment. Everything was on schedule and with fewer than two hours left to go, I was confident (probably too confident) that crew scheduling wasn't going to need me. But if they summoned me, I was ready to cut my date short and race back to the terminal as if I'd been there the whole time. It was a little risky, but I wanted something else to do besides sit around in the crew lounge watching Netflix on a Friday night.

Jean Charles and I had been trying to coordinate our busy schedules for several weeks. An accountant and real estate developer from Haiti now living in the United States, he was pleasant enough on the phone and sounded normal. He didn't live far and was game for meeting me at the airport for dinner. I appreciated his understanding of my situation and its uncertainty. He encouraged the waiter to bring our food quickly, along with his second glass of wine. We were off to such a great start.

After ordering, we talk more about our lives, our interests, and our past relationships.

"Okay, so your turn. Tell me about your last relationship," I asked after briefly sharing about the difficulties of dating over the past few months.

"Well, I've been divorced for a while, but I'm ready for something serious again."

"May I ask how long it's been?"

"Almost a year," he said as our waiter approached to check on us. "Yes, I'll have another glass please."

His face tensed after responding to my inquiry and I didn't see the need to pry any further. But, as the waiter brought Jean Charles a third glass of wine, he volunteered the details without prompting.

"We were married for five years and she cheated on me several times," he continued. Over his third glass of wine, and while we ate, he continued about his wife and her affair. His magnetic eyes dimmed as he talked on and on, nostalgically looking off into the distance over my shoulder.

"His name was Pierre. I can't believe it! He was at our wedding and had given us this fancy espresso machine."

I tripled-checked my phone to make sure I hadn't missed any calls from scheduling. An hour to go until I officially finished my standby shift. I quickly declined dessert as Jean Charles ordered and gulped his fifth glass of wine while he described the features of the espresso machine that he enjoyed learning how to use. I really didn't know what to say, so I just nodded and kept listening. I wondered if perhaps Netflix would have been the better choice.

The date got more awkward as tears began welling up in his eyes while he told me that he had decided to keep the espresso maker when she moved out. The waiter finally brought him the check. My airport shift and the date were over.

Jean Charles slightly stumbled as he got up from his seat to order an Uber. I suggested we share one that dropped him off first so that I could make sure he got home safely. Once in the Uber, Jean Charles nodded off. I nudged him when we arrived at his house ten minutes later.

"I had a good time," he said, yawning.

"Me too," I lied.

The next day, Jean Charles texted me with an apology. He admitted he probably drank too much because he was so nervous about our date. Would I give him a chance to make it up to me? Although his behavior was bizarre, I could understand being nervous. I agreed to go out with him again.

We went out to dinner and several times after. He was a foodie and loved checking out new restaurants. He never had more than one glass of wine. We had meaningful conversations on topics other than his failed marriage, and most importantly we laughed a lot. I was starting to like Jean Charles more and more with each date. He definitely had the qualities that I was looking for in a mate. He was a good listener, upbeat, and genuinely interested in us getting to know one another. I was pretty sure too he wasn't an alcoholic.

For three weeks, Jean Charles and I texted each other every couple of days. We'd coordinate the logistics for our next dinner date usually once or twice a week when I was in town. Sometimes, we'd just text to see how the other was doing after a busy day. One evening, I texted Jean Charles, but didn't hear back. It was unusual not to get a text reply within a few minutes. After three days, I texted him again; "All is well?" No reply. I called and got his voicemail. "Um, are we still on for dinner tomorrow?"

"Not sure what's happened, but hope you're okay," was the last text I sent.

I checked his Facebook page for clues. Had he been in an accident? Death in the family? The last picture posted was a day ago. A photo of the setting sun on the lakefront with a caption reading, "my morning walk." I clicked the "like" button, pretending it was a middle finger instead of a thumb.

He wasn't dead; he had simply ghosted me.

I replayed the last date in our head. I reviewed our entire string of text conversations. My girlfriends assured me that it wasn't anything I did.

One month later, I got a text from Jean Charles with an apology. The night after our last date, he had learned that his ex-wife was getting remarried. He hadn't taken the news too well and was recovering emotionally. He hoped to someday see me again when he was doing better.

I didn't reply.

Brandon and I met downtown at a happy hour one night. I thought he and I had some potential for something long term. But, after a few months of frequently seeing each other, he crinkled his nose in disdain and scrunched his thick black eyebrows when I asked if we were exclusive.

"Uh uh, that ain't for me," he said as if I asked him if he wanted pickles on a hamburger.

Brandon was new to town when we first met. He had relocated to Chicago for a new job as an HR manager at a manufacturing plant. Cute, funny, and smart, he and I were from the same hometown with a lot in common. His witty, sarcastic sense of humor matched my own.

We spent a lot of time together before and after my trips, texted each other daily with politically incorrect jokes, and laughed at the absurdities of our work. He frequently picked me up from the airport and I always brought him silly souvenirs from my travels. There were memorable winter weekends spent cooped up at his place, marveling at how neither one of us annoyed the other in such cramped quarters. We talked about our families and our life goals, but in hindsight, we really didn't talk about relationship goals. I just assumed that he and I were on the same page as things between us were always easy. But at that moment when I asked about exclusivity, it was clear that we were not.

"Okaaaay, fair enough, " I said calmly. "So, what are we?" In that moment, I was surprised more than I was hurt.

"Friends with benefits?"

"Uh uh, that's really not for me."

"You're right," he said. "*Really* good friends with benefits?" I was getting pissed but tried not to show it.

"Sure, buddy," I replied curtly.

Work got unusually busy. That's what I told Brandon anyway. When he offered to pick me up, I let him know I really didn't need a ride from the airport; I was taking the train home. Dinner? I just ate. Coming over? I was tired and had an early check-in. Lots of errands to run. I wasn't sure when I'd be back to town. My text responses were polite, but short. I didn't have any more funny passenger stories to share. For days, I didn't have a response to the set-up of the punch line of his jokes. This was after I told him more than once that perhaps we could be friends at a later date. I understood that he enjoyed being a bachelor but, in the meantime,, I needed space.

Brandon didn't take the hint, or rather he didn't want to. I knew he enjoyed our friendship. We'd grown used to each other's company and talking at least once every day. He didn't make our non-breakup breakup easy. He kept calling and texting despite my polite requests that he stop. The more I thought about it, I was hurt, mad, and disappointed. I really liked Brandon and I had feelings for him, but I wanted more than he offered from our "friendship."

"Oh, so don't call you, you'll call me?" he said snarkily.

"Yeah, something like that. Thanks for understanding," I said, my voice dripping with sarcasm.

"Take all the time you need."

I was relieved. He finally got it.

Two days later, Brandon sent a text.

Hey, how's it going?

Instead of replying, I changed my phone settings and blocked his number.

BLOG POST: THANKS ON A PLANE

Chi McFly | August 5, 2016 | Released To Crew Rest

As a flight attendant, dealing with passenger shenanigans is inevitable. It runs the gamut from whining and pouting to obnoxious outbursts. And no, I'm not talking about the children on the plane. The problem passengers are usually fully grown adults who, for some reason, lose their damn minds and common sense when they get on the plane.

While I have endless and entertaining "You won't believe what this passenger did" stories, I don't wish to focus on those all the time. There are already enough websites related to passenger shaming and flight attendant rants. On social media, you can always find a plethora of passenger complaints about uncaring flight attendants and delayed flights. Then, there is also the news media which fuels and exaggerates airplane occurrences that often paint the picture of a big-bad airline company and its evil legion of flight attendants.

Now that I'm working in the business, I do pay a little bit more attention to these stories, but not much. I know there's always more to the story than what's reported. In the age where complaining can garner negative publicity and free tickets, expressing dissatisfaction in the form of outrage and posting it on social media pays off. I understand it, but I don't necessarily condone it.

But rather than re-hashing hearsay and speculating on what really happened, I've tried to understand why people behave the way they do – especially on a plane. I'm not a psychology expert by any means, but I've always had an interest in the topic. For practical purposes, my hope is, at the very least, knowing the "why" can yield a few hours of peace on a plane so I can get through a flight without having to write an incident report.

So, after a couple of years in the business, I try to keep in mind these reasons when I'm frequently dealing with certain types of passengers:

1. People are ineffective at dealing with stress. To start, many people generally don't handle stress too well. For infrequent travelers, the stress of preparation while managing regular day-to-day activities quickly gets to be overwhelming. For those who don't frequently travel by plane, navigating constantly changing airport security regulations and airline nuances is such an unfamiliar experience, especially for those who thrive on predictability. Leaving the familiarity of home and coordinating everything it takes to be gone for several days or weeks is something most people have not learned. So, they pack up their stress and anxieties, but somehow manage to walk out their front door without manners.

2. Others just lack situational awareness. It's human nature to focus on one's self, and it's easy to forget that 150-plus people are flying with you on the same aircraft. Those individuals have also experienced the same pre-travel stress that you have, as have your flight attendants, who were also delayed and had to drag bags to the airport as well.

But, that's why flight attendants exist. To direct passengers to the seats that are listed on their smartphones, printed on their tickets, and labeled on the aircraft. We also remind them that there are others behind them or in front of them, waiting to sit down too. I tend to have more patience for the clueless ones. Yes, while it can still be annoying, these passengers with manners are often apologetic and compliant once I point out that I cannot walk through them if they are standing up and blocking the entire aisle.

3. And then there are the assholes waiting for an opportunity to act out. Some people, no matter where they are or, if they're well-rested or sleep-deprived, they are going to choose to be assholes. No, I don't think they're born this way, but perhaps something happened to them way back when (or, even as recently as the security line), and they haven't let it go. Unfortunately for flight attendants, they then decide to get on our airplane and they're looking for something to go wrong so they can complain. While at times, their complaint may be valid, how they choose to complain usually makes the situation worse rather than better.

Cultivating compassion for myself and for others is one of my personal goals. I think it's something I see missing on the plane and in this world in general. It's missing among passengers and sometimes among flight attendants. I really think that it should be a life skill that's taught in schools, alongside cultural awareness and basic communication skills.

In the meantime, I will do what I can, say "no" with a smile, and tell those that refuse to comply that they can either take the next flight or we can happily arrange for security to resolve the matter when we land.

ADVENTURES IN BABYSITTING

F ortunately, very few situations require the involvement of security. Many can be solved with drinks and a snack. This one particular situation dealing with a persistent passenger comes to mind:

It was 12:35 a.m. and after an eight-hour weather delay, our flight to Baltimore boarded. I greet weary passengers with a resigned "Hello, again" and an unspoken look that says "I'm tired too and ready to go home."

We take off, reach our cruising altitude, and prepare for service. We keep the ceiling lights off and move about quietly. A flight attendant call bell chimes, indicating a request from a passenger in the cabin. I carefully head up the dark aisle to answer it. On my left and right as I'm walking down the aisle are passengers asleep with their heads thrown back against headrests and mouths hanging open. Others are huddled up against windows, wrapped in blankets.

Near the back of the plane, the row with a flight attendant call light illuminated overhead appears to be empty. As I walk closer, two small children occupy the seats. I can barely make out their small faces attempting to peer over their seat backs, but can easily see the whites of their little eyes. Both of them are wide awake.

As I suspected, the call light belongs to the same little boy, about eight years old, who had asked for headphones for the TV right after I went through offering headphones to every single person before takeoff. He's sitting next to his sister, who looks about the same age. Her eyes are glued to the TV monitor in front of her.

"May I have a Sprite?" he politely asks.

"It will be just a few minutes. We're still getting set up," I whisper softly not to wake the other passengers around us.

"Oh, okay," he says as his sister quickly glances up at me from the adjacent seat and then back at the movie on her monitor.

A few minutes later, I'm walking backwards up the aisle, pulling the heavy drink cart to the front of the plane as my coworker pushes. Out of the corner of my eye, I see the boy waving his hand high from his middle seat to flag me down.

I know what he wants.

"Hold on," I tell him firmly while holding up my finger without stopping. "We're coming."

When we reach his row, I serve the boy his Sprite and his sister asks for a Sprite as well. A few minutes later as we're finishing up service, his call button chimes again. I sigh and head back out to answer it. He politely asks if there are any snacks.

"We have them, but you have to buy them," I explain. By this time, with my own fatigue sneaking up on me, I'm a little bit annoyed. "Where are your parents?" I ask.

He points across the aisle. I turn to see a man and a woman sleeping. Their seat backs are fully reclined. The woman's head is resting on the man's shoulder. Sprawled between the two is a sleeping toddler sucking his thumb. All three are clearly passed out from exhaustion.

Without saying a word, I head back to the galley and get the button-happy boy some snacks. I instruct him to share with his sister in the same tone I use with my six-year-old niece and nephew.

"Are they free?" he asks.

I lean over and assure the boy that the snacks are free.

"And you see that button right there?" I continue, leaning over and pointing up to the button that's become his best friend.

"Don't ever ring it again. If you need something else, just wait. We'll be back by in a few minutes, okay?"

He nods in solemn understanding. I nod back in approval.

My two favorite passengers of the flight go back to quietly watching their movie until landing.

One would think ad hoc babysitting duties as a flight attendant entails taking care of other people's children, but the need to intervene in childish arguments between adults occurs with more frequency. Take this one for example:

I'm standing in the aisle at my assigned position as the safety video plays before take-off. It's my third and final flight of the day. The plane is packed full with passengers and their carry-on luggage that was a nightmare to properly stow.

A middle-aged woman, sitting in a middle seat, two rows in front of where I'm standing, yells out. She's arguing with the passenger next to her, also a middle-aged woman, who is in the aisle seat next to her.

"Is everything okay?" I ask both passengers with concern.

"She's putting her arm in my space," explains the woman sitting in the aisle as she points out the space next to her arm.

"I have a right to put my arm here," declares the middle-seat woman.

They. Are. Fighting. Over. The. Armrest.

I'm tired. My job is to help with safety checks and medical emergencies such as the one on the previous flight where a passenger fainted from dehydration after partying all night in Las Vegas. I don't do armrest disputes. Not today.

"We have two hours and thirty-eight minutes in the air. If you two can't work it out, we will have to go back to the gate right now or divert the flight," I calmly explain.

They continue to bicker, but at a softer level. I repeat myself a bit louder.

Silence.

One woman grudgingly looks to her left out the window; the other looks down at her hands in her lap. Both women are trying to ignore me.

At this point, I'm confused because I'm pretty sure the two women are well over the age of twelve and I look at them with disbelief.

"Excuse me ladies, do you understand what I'm saying? I need some type of response."

"Yes," they feebly mutter as they glance up and then quickly away.

"Thank you," I state firmly before walking away. A passenger two rows behind me snickers.

I inform the lead flight attendant of "the situation." Together, we check in on the women to reinforce the gravity and pettiness of the disagreement.

They are both silent and scowling.

Several minutes later as I walk to my jumpseat in the back of the plane, the middle-seat woman looks up and gives me the evil eye. I stare directly back and send her a telepathic message to quit acting like a fool.

Our flight takes off. We reach our destination on time. I have no idea and little concern about who won the armrest war.

BLOG POST: JETWAY JESUS

Chi McFly | October 27, 2016| Released To Crew Rest

There are passengers who request a wheelchair that takes them to the front of the security line. The wheelchair-assisted passengers are also first to board the plane before first class passengers. From time to time, there are wheelchair passengers that don't need one to get off when the plane lands – only to board. Rather than remain seated and wait for the wheelchair to arrive, they sometimes grab their luggage and quickly walk all the way up the jetway bridge that was so difficult to walk down. As the last to disembark, flight attendants joke amongst ourselves as we past the awaiting empty chairs on the jet bridge that it's a miracle – Jetway Jesus has healed once again.

ACT II

FLASHBACK: MY MOTHER'S KEEPER

When I was sixteen, my mother said half-jokingly that daughters are supposed to take care of their aging mothers.

A moody teen longing for independence, I scoffed at such an idea. What about my brother? He could live his life freely and I would be forever chained, limited in the possibilities of my life based on my mother's health?

Long before I knew travel would be a big part of my life, I resented what I felt was an archaic and unfair notion. As I got older and found myself still in Michigan for college, the desire for independence, to get out of the state, grew stronger. It was never that I didn't enjoy being with family or that I wanted to run away and never come back. I just really wanted a chance to leave and explore the world I had read so much about in the many books I consumed. I knew so many people who were born and raised in Michigan, (my mother included), who never left.

For whatever reason, financial or family obligations, they lived and worked in the same place where they were born. I didn't want that to be me.

I was at college, finishing up my senior year and getting excited about my upcoming study abroad when my mother called to tell me she was in the hospital. She sounded okay, but said she hadn't been feeling well for the past few days. Only an hour from home, I drove to see her the same afternoon. I wouldn't be surprised if it was stress. It was not the first time she had worried herself sick.

In all fairness, my mother took on a lot. Growing up, my mother embodied the "strong Black woman:" she was always working full-time and raising two kids on her own as a single mother. She was firm, yet fair, demanding a lot of her children and from herself – especially when it came to our education. Twenty years later, my brother and I were in college and she was an award-winning middle school science teacher in one of the toughest urban neighborhoods. Over the past several years, with growing responsibilities at her job, she also worked as a freelance education consultant and mentored teachers throughout the country. With my brother and I away from home, she frequently traveled the country to teachers' conferences and wrote grant proposals. In the summer months, for as long as I can remember, she and my aunt baked and sold pies. During tax season, she did other people's tax returns.

That afternoon when I arrived at the hospital, Pat (my older cousin and my mom's best friend) was already there with her. They had moved her from the emergency department to a regular inpatient room. The three of us sat around waiting for her test results. Other than a bit tired, she looked okay to me.

A few hours later, a doctor came into the room. A middle-aged white man with a reassuring smile, he introduced himself and took a seat on the rolling stool. He switched on the x-ray light and pinned the films of my mother's heart on the wall. He informed us that the pain and fatigue she had been experiencing for quite some time was due to multiple blockages in her heart. She had experienced a mild heart attack, but fortunately, they caught it in time. The doctor went on casually to say that she would need bypass surgery to clear the arteries. It was a common procedure, but a heart surgery nonetheless.

I blinked back the tears from my eyes. There was no need for such dramatics I told myself. My mother would be fine. I would just need to reassure her of that to make sure she wouldn't stress herself out even more. Besides, the doctor just said it was a fairly routine procedure, and with her age of fifty-two, they didn't anticipate any problems. She would, however, have to quit smoking.

Over the next few days, my brother flew in from North Carolina along with my aunt from Las Vegas and both my uncles from Atlanta and San Diego. My grandparents were also there for the procedure. This was becoming a big deal as we all sat around in the hospital waiting room.

As I figured, everything went fine. She was awake and talking not too long after the procedure. The recovery process, although not lengthy, would be a process. She'd be in the hospital for a few days and was then instructed to take it easy for a few weeks at home. During her hospital stay, I suggested that I postpone my plans to study abroad in South Africa and stay home to help her with the recovery. I could go next semester.

"No, baby," she said. "You don't need to do that. I'll be fine."

I was reluctant about doing so, but she was insistent.

I felt guilty and at the same time relieved. I really wanted to go.

A few days later, my mother was released from the hospital. My brother and I headed back to school. I drove back on weekends to check on her.

When the time arrived for me to head to South Africa, she was almost back to normal but moved a bit slower than before. Off from full-time teaching in the summer, my mother went back to work teaching part-time, but no longer traveling. The family had a bit of a scare, but as I already knew, my mother was invincible. I could get back to my life and head to South Africa without worry.

RESERVES ANONYMOUS

When I first started working for the airlines, Anna warned me that my first year or so would be tough since I'd probably be what's called a reserve flight attendant[11] with little seniority. This meant I wouldn't be able to choose when or where I would fly and would have only few off days each month. But, the company was in a hiring frenzy and the more flight attendants they hired, the faster I would move up the list in seniority which was based on my hire date. More seniority, meaning the longer a flight attendant has been with the company in comparison to others, meant less time on reserve. Eventually, I'd get regular schedule like the one Anna had. I'd be what they called a line holder. As a line holder, I could then

---

11 A reserve flight attendant is a on call flight attendant that must be readily available often on short notice. Reserves are typically new hires having been employed by the company for the least amount of time.

pick and choose from available trips. I'd have more flexibility as to how many and which days I wanted to work each month.

"If you can survive reserve, you'll eventually be a line holder and can have more control over your life," she said.

Two and a half years later, although the company was still hiring, they were hiring slowly. So, in the middle of every month, when all flight attendants "bid" or requested their preferred schedule for the next month, although I requested a regular line, I always got stuck with reserve because of my seniority. On award day, my schedule would simply show what days I was on call (also called on duty) and what days I was off. As a reserve, I rarely got the days off I wanted or needed, so I'd have trade days off with other reserves. But everyone wanted the holidays and weekends off which made it more difficult. Being a reserve meant that I sometimes missed weddings, funerals, and birthdays because I couldn't get the days off.

But there were a lot of flight attendants on reserve and we tried to make the best of it by supporting one another. When alcohol and music were missing, there was still laughter wherever we were: at the hotel, on the plane, and even in the employee crew lounge.

Our employee crew lounge is like a doctor's waiting room, except larger. Spaced throughout the carpeted area, along the walls, under dimmed fluorescent lights are small clusters of petite pleather lounge chairs, ottomans, sofas, and small tables. In one corner, there's a coffee machine, refrigerator, and sink. In the other are computer terminals and worktables. Outside the space to the left is a small storage room for luggage. Sometimes, there's another room with cots for sleeping. To the right is a changing room and vanity table with basic grooming supplies such as hair spray, nail files, and lint rollers. The space is far from posh, but comfortable enough. Quieter than the terminal hallways, it's where flight attendants congregate and wait.

It was the middle of the day on a slow Wednesday. Ten to fifteen reserves were on airport standby for the past two hours and the phone hadn't rung once. [12] Flight operations for the day were running smoothly. There weren't yet any weather or mechanical delays. No one had called in sick. In fact, it was unusually quiet and relaxed in the lounge.

After about two-and-a-half hours of sitting around, the group of reserves that had started their shift at around noon had grown tired of sleeping, reading, watching Netflix, and whatever else we were doing. The noise level picked up as we all took a break from our solitude to chat. We all knew one another, as we all had been hired at around the same time. We'd either worked together or saw each other around the base or in the bars and clubs in Wicker Park. It wasn't intentional, but as we sat around chatting, we noticed that our chairs had been haphazardly arranged in a circle as if it was planned.

"Well," I said in jest as if I were a schoolteacher gathering the kindergartners for story time. "I'd like to welcome everyone to Reserves Anonymous. Let's go around the room and introduce ourselves."

Everyone started laughing and playing along. We pulled our chairs closer into a formal circle.

"My name is Rose and I'm ... " She paused reluctantly. " ... a reserve." She hung her head in shame.

Others gasped in horror. Someone mockingly patted her on the back. There was a sympathetic patter of applause. The rest of us were cracking up.

"My name is Brit, and I'm a reserve."

---

12 In this reference, flight attendants are assigned to go to the airport in uniform and their bags packed to "standby" in case they are needed at the last minute to work a flight due to the originally scheduled flight attendant being unavailable for a variety of reasons (i.e., sick, missed connection, etc.).

"I'm Alex, I like Doritos, long walks on the beach, and sleeping in late. I'm a reserve!"

"Carol, and yes, I'm a reserve."

"Tell us about your experience on reserve. We're listening," I said to Carol.

"One time, I was at the salon, getting my nails done, I was thinking about getting a pedicure and then, the phone rang. I wasn't able to get my toes done!"

"*Noooo!*"

We shook our heads in dismay. I nodded to Brit to go next.

"I made plans to meet up with my friend for lunch and – "

"You made *plans*?" I screamed in a confrontational tone. "You should have known better! You're a reserve, dammit!"

"I stayed up late because I really wanted to finish a movie. I mean, it's not like I got an assignment, or I was number ten on the list - they probably weren't going to use me. So, I went to bed at two in the morning"

"Tsk, Tsk."

"They called me at three a.m. for a five a.m. flight!" Alex broke down in fake sobs and fell out of the chair onto his knees.

By now, everyone including me was belly-laughing at our antics. We were trying to catch our breath and keep the shenanigans going. We'd all been there – looking forward to plans but knowing there was a possibility we'd have to cancel at the last minute. Not sleeping, and when we finally do, being startled from sleep by a three a.m. call. We all had to deal with insanely long delays and never-ending flights. We laughed out of recognition of our behaviors and the impossible circumstances we often found ourselves in as reserves. Although we knew better, we'd try to predict when we would and wouldn't be assigned a trip on the days we were on duty. We fell for the illusion that we had some control over our lives.

A bright red rotary-dial telephone in the corner of the room rang sharply. The "bat phone" we called it. It was a direct line to and from crew scheduling. We all turned at the same time to look. We watched as Alex left our circle to answer it. He called out two last names and two members of our group left the circle to gather by the phone for the assignment details.

"A 2-day Boise[13]," Alex said out loud as he rolled his eyes. The three assigned grabbed their bags and headed from the lounge to the terminal.

Our reserve support group disbanded.

A month later, I sat on the sofa in my therapist's office, blowing snot from my nose into a mound of tissue and wiping my eyes before continuing. It was mid-spring, and the start of my third year as a flight attendant. Life as a reserve hadn't gotten any easier. It had gotten worse.

"I'm just so tired all of the time," I wailed.

"Our layovers are so short I can't get enough sleep after working thirteen-hour days. With summer travel starting again, it's going to get worse," I explained.

Bethany, the therapist, listened and nodded. A short, brown-haired white woman, she was nice enough but rarely helpful.

"Everyone is out enjoying the spring, running along the lakefronts, and attending street festivals, and all I'm doing is either going to work or just getting off – too tired to do anything."

During my four-day stints on reserve, if I was lucky to be home at all during those four days, I was given exactly ten hours of crew rest before being called back to do it all over again. I

13   A work trip lasting two days with a layover in Boise, Idaho

was flying well above the average monthly flight hours for the past two months.

I should have been off reserve by now. There was a gradual decline, and then a halt to the hiring frenzy that Anna had predicted. Business was good for the airlines, but it wasn't that good, I guess. Months after I started, I gave up trying to predict when I wouldn't get used or the company's rationale for their ever-changing business strategy. I was a frontline soldier. I had survived a full year of sleep deprivation and random colds from germs floating around in recycled cabin air. I was now going into my third year.

"I don't know how much longer I can do this. I try to make plans and always have to cancel."

I was also tired frequently and often unable to sleep soundly for fear I would miss a phone call from scheduling.

The new friends I was making in Chicago didn't bother calling anymore because they assumed I was out of town. I thought my problems would be solved when I got a full-time job. Sure, I had a small, steady paycheck, but nothing more. Could I really handle being on reserve indefinitely? This was not the jet-setting life I had envisioned. I was moving further away instead of closer to my vision of being a location-independent entrepreneur. My entire life revolved around flying to pay bills.

After going on and on, Bethany, who I had been seeing over the past few months to help manage the growing stress, was once again not offering any solutions. She mainly just listened with intensity.

"What do you think you should do?" she inquired when she finished jotting on her note pad.

"I don't know. Quit maybe?"

"You could, but will you be happier if you're unable to travel?"

"I'll be happier if I'm able to sleep."

As usual, I didn't leave the therapist's office with any answers – just more questions. After sharing my frustrations though, I felt better. I would have to do something different. There was a decision I would eventually have to make: could I continue indefinitely a life of such uncertainty for the sake of travel benefits I could never really use? How long would I be willing to sacrifice my time, energy, or health for a paycheck? I thought I knew what I signed up for, but reserve life was taking its toll.

Spring flowers were in full bloom as I left the building to catch the train back home. I realized it was the twentieth of the month. *My schedule for the upcoming month should be out by now.* I checked my phone. The best I could hope for would be a reserve schedule with a few weekend days off. I typed in my employee number and hit enter.

My awarded schedule for the month popped up. For the first time, I had specific trips and destinations on the calendar.

I was now a line holder.

LIVING MY LIFE
LIKE A LINE HOLDER

L ine holder life, as compared to reserve, was a completely different world. Finally, I had more freedom, flexibility, and control over my schedule.

Although I was assigned each month a regular line with red-eye flights and weekend trips, it didn't matter.[14] From the comfort of home or a hotel room on my computer, I could easily give away my trips to other flight attendants or trade them for better ones. Most of the time, I could get weekends off when I wanted. I could pick how many hours I wanted to work each month, which could be a little or a lot, each month, depending on how much money I wanted.

Every now and then, I snagged an international assignment. In the summer months, fewer senior flight attendants, who had

---

14   The least desirable schedules are given to new line holders who are no longer reserve flight attendants.

the ability to hold international lines, wanted to work. So, they'd frequently give away their trips at the last minute. Usually in the late evenings, the day before the scheduled trip, an alert would pop up on my phone, notifying me that an international trip was available.

During my first summer as a line holder, I picked up assignments to Venice, Barcelona, Amsterdam, and Zurich. For me, international trips were like mini-vacations. It was one leg over to get there, a twenty-four-hour layover, and then one leg back. I was dead tired when I returned from long flights and jet-lagged, but it was always worth it to explore someplace new. Plus, since international trips paid more than domestic flights, I usually made enough money to cover what I spent shopping for souvenirs.

Once again, flight attendant life was exciting and new. I could think straight, plan better, and most importantly, I could sleep in a lot more often. The anxiety of missing a call should I oversleep was gone. I didn't always have to keep my phone attached to my side. Finally, I knew where I was going at least a day or two in advance and when I would return.

With this new freedom, I started going out more when I was in town and enjoying the Chicago summer, like a real person who actually lived there. There were concerts, street festivals, and farmer's markets. I committed to weekly photography classes and volunteered regularly as a mentor for teenage girls.

I could tell my friends and family when I would be around. I rarely canceled at the last minute, and if I did, it wasn't really due to work (although, on rare occasions, I could say it was). I was able to hang out enough to see the same people again and make friends. Every now and then, I played host to several international flight attendants from other airlines. I spent time with my cousins in Hyde Park, like we used to do before I moved there. I went to plays and restaurants with Marsha and Miguel.

Mike, although working most of the time, was still around and we'd go out from time to time. Occasionally, I met up with other flight-attendant friends from my company. My brother and sister-in-law officially relocated from Atlanta to a suburb in Chicago, which meant I could see my niece and nephew more often. I babysat and randomly attended their baseball games and soccer practices. I went to weddings and a few funerals out of town.

My dating life improved, too. I put more effort into online dating and met a few interesting guys. Although most of the guys were not relationship material, they too wanted companionship to get out and explore the city, especially during the summer. With Charlie, I biked along the lakefront to Buckingham Fountain at night. I went kayaking on Lake Michigan with Ben and hiking at Starved Rock with Antonio.

I had a job, a social life, and energy to focus on getting back to my entrepreneurial endeavors. Wanting to keep my writing skills sharp and make extra money, I started blogging more about my layovers while helping others with their book projects. Although employed full-time, I controlled my work schedule like an hourly contractor. I was able to give myself enough time between trips to fully rest and recover before hitting the skies again.

Going into my fourth year, my hourly salary only slightly increased. But now, if I wanted or needed to, I could fly more and earn extra money. I hadn't yet made enough money to move into an apartment of my own, but I was able to pay down my credit card bills. I even saved up enough money to buy a cheap used car.

I'd been told by many more-experienced flight attendants that life as a line holder and life as a reserve would be as different as night and day. They were right. After almost three years of constant uncertainty, sticking it out to be a line holder was worth it.

A RAINY NIGHT IN LONDON

During takeoff, I sat at the single jumpseat by the front galley exit door and planned it all out. A quick nap after this red-eye flight from Chicago to London and I'd be good to go. True, this plan had never worked out like that before, but I was determined to make the most of my twenty-four-hour layover. This would be my third time in the city that, to me, was like a remixed version of New York – an international hub with so much to see and do.

Throughout the flight, I networked with the crew to find out what everyone else was doing. There were nine flight attendants; all senior to me in years of employment, and all of them regularly flew back and forth to London. Several mentioned they were thinking about going to a nearby pub, a few were going to the mall, and Mildred, (age seventy, the most senior of the crew in age and years of employment) was ordering room service for her dinner and going to sleep.

On previous trips, I visited shopping malls and seen all the tourist sites. I didn't want to sit around at a pub with the crew. If Shona hadn't moved to Madrid to start her career as a teacher, I'd probably be catching up with her again. But, after talking with everyone, I realized that if I wanted to do something different, I'd have to strike out on my own. In the United States, I went out by myself on layovers every now and then. But, I was still nervous to go off the beaten path and venture totally solo overseas.

Seven hours and two time zones later, we touched down in London. Dense gray clouds and strong winds foreshadowing rain welcomed us to Heathrow. Back in Chicago, it was 5 a.m. Fatigue and jet lag gnawed away at my desire to do anything. By the time the crew van delivered us to the hotel, water poured from the sky, making it perfect for staying indoors and sleeping the day away. A steady beat of raindrops drummed against my hotel room window as I happily tucked myself in underneath the soft feather comforter on the king-size bed. I convinced myself that a few hours instead of a few minutes of sleep wouldn't derail my plans as long as I woke up by 5 p.m.

I woke up from a deep sleep at 6:30 p.m., feeling as if I had been mowed down by a boulder that was still pinned on top of me. Before I could think about it, and with all the mental strength I could muster, I catapulted myself from the bed into the shower to shock myself awake. I found my fierce resolve after two cups of instant espresso I made with hot water from the room's electric kettle. I was doubtful that I would find anything to do on a damp Wednesday night and thought about just going to meet up with the crew for dinner in a few minutes. The dull gray skies were getting darker as I sat down at the tiny hotel room desk. If I didn't find anything of interest, I'd just hang with my lame crew and try to make the best of it. I opened my laptop to consult my trusted friend Google.

Search box query attempt number one inquiring where to find Black people in London yielded only weekend events. The second search box query asking about "Things to Do in London" listed all the tourist stuff I'd already done. My third query about "Fun Events in London Tonight" gave me a few options...

I second and triple-guessed my decision to go as I put on a pair of jeans and a long-sleeved knit shirt. I ignored my doubt, grabbed my umbrella, and headed to the nearby Tube station as the rain started up again. Forty-five minutes and two Tube transfers later, a drizzle persisted as I walked a couple of blocks through a bustling urban neighborhood of cafes and shops in South London. People with black and brown faces, finishing up their after-work errands, strode past me in both directions, trying to outpace another inevitable rain shower approaching.

After a few minutes and a few wrong turns, I arrived in front of a two-story brick building that matched the Google maps picture on my phone, right before it started raining. Upbeat, syncopated rhythms of steel drums and Cuban horns guided me up the narrow flight of wooden stairs at the building's entrance. I was halfway hoping not to find the location. That way, I could go back to the hotel and get back in bed, knowing that I tried. But at the top of the stairs I found D'Santos Salsa class and Dance party. I couldn't let my nerves get the best of me now. With this weather though, I figured there probably wouldn't even be a lot of people there. Either way, I already decided I wasn't going to stay long.

I walked into the spacious, brightly lit ballroom. There was a diverse and respectable-sized crowd of about thirty people. Men and women of all ages scattered around the room listened to the dance instructor at the front. He was a petite man with sandy brown hair who commanded the space, wearing a fitted dress shirt, equally tight slacks, and a Panama straw hat. His assistant, an attractive Middle Eastern looking woman clad in a sexy, red, flared dress and high platform heels wandered the room, correcting postures and hand placements of couples as they paired up. Although several people were wearing jeans, I suddenly felt underdressed. In one corner, a DJ was awaiting his cue to turn the music on and off. In the other was a bartender, serving drinks behind a small bar. I paid my fifteen pounds to the smiling woman who greeted me at the door. She informed me that the bachata class was wrapping up and I could join in for the salsa class at the next break.

I sat in a chair off to the side of the dance floor and watched nervously. I knew from previous lessons in my past that dancing (anything regarding coordination, really) was not one of my strengths. But, that never stopped me from trying. Every year or so, when invited by a friend in Atlanta, Chicago, or wherever I lived, I attended a random dance class or two, hoping to master a simplified step sequence. I never did, but if I didn't step on anyone's toes too hard, the lesson, although embarrassing, was tolerable. This time, I hoped, would be different.

The instructor counted down and pointed to the DJ to cue the music. A steady Afro-Latin beat at a moderate volume played from the speakers and the paired-off students began spinning and twirling to the instructor's count. One, two, three, four. One, two, three, four. Some of the couples flowed across the floor with ease while others awkwardly shuffled left and right.

After a few minutes of practice, the instructor cued the DJ to stop the music and called everyone to line up in rows on the dance floor. Even though it was the bachata class, I joined the group as instructed, along with several others who were sitting and standing along the dance floor. As soon as everyone was on the floor, the lights went off without warning and multicolored strobe lights flickered on, instantly transforming the ballroom into a nightclub. A loud thumping bass replaced the soft, timed beats and the instructor led the group in an Afro-Latin version of the Cupid Shuffle. *Oh, I know this one.* I twirled my hips, waved my arms, and kicked my legs out with confidence. Five minutes later, the dance party ended with everyone sweating and giving each other congratulatory booty bumps. A bit more relaxed, I was ready to salsa!

After a short break, the lights went up again and the salsa lessons started. The beginner students were paired off with the intermediate students. My partner, a friendly older Black gentleman who was a few inches shorter than me introduced himself as Don. Together, we watched as the instructor guided us on hand placement and foot movement. I grinned nervously at Don as I placed my hand in his and as his other hand lightly rested on my waist. I mirrored his relaxed posture. I warned Don that I was really bad.

"No worry, gurrl," he assured me in an accent that sounded part Jamaican and part British. "I'll show you! Where you from?"

I told him that I'm visiting from Chicago as the music cued up. By the count of three, I was already lost.

"Look up and jus' follow where I move," Don said patiently.

I resisted the urge to look down at my feet. I stared at Don, who was smiling and giving me an encouraging nod while counting. I was shuffling rather than stepping and pretty sure I was doing it wrong. I stepped on his feet multiple times, losing the count every time I apologized. I felt bad for Don, to be matched with a partner who can barely keep the beat, but he didn't seem to mind that I kept stumbling and frequently twirling the wrong way. *No matter the location, guess I still suck,* I thought to myself.

The class ended and the lights went down again. The dance party started up and went on for the rest of the night. I thanked Don for bearing with me and I headed to the bar for water before making a beeline back to the row of chairs on the side of the dance floor to people-watch. I envied the dancers, including Don, who had found another partner, one that better matched his skill level.

I sat alone and enjoyed the music. I was feeling awkward sitting by myself, and it seemed as if everyone knew everyone else. A few chairs over were two young guys in their twenties, chatting with one another. I smiled and joined in.

"Do you guys come to this class often?" I asked.

"Not really, but every now and then, my mom makes me come with her for the class. It's fun and she likes it," one guy said, pointing to the dance floor to a woman that looked only slightly older than him. She was dancing with another male student from the class.

The two friends, Kyle and Richard, inquired about where I was from. Soon, we were talking about life in the United States and their hopes to visit someday. I was relieved my accent was apparently a good ice-breaker. Kyle's mom came off the dance floor and sat with us to relax. She was equally friendly and welcomed me when Kyle mentioned that I was visiting from Chicago.

A few minutes later, Don stepped off the dance floor and headed toward me. I was certain he wanted nothing to do with the tall clumsy girl until he held out his hand for me to join him on the floor. To my surprise and delight, we continued practicing. Enamored with the music, Don was moving his feet and hips with the expert precision of a long-time student. He had the ease and grace of a Chicago stepper. His joy was infectious, and eventually, I stopped worrying about if I was doing it right.

Following his lead, I moved my hips and glided my feet, stepping forward, back, and then forward again. I soon found myself twirling in the right direction and mimicking Don's carefree air. As we danced, Don talked about what side of town he was from and why coming weekly was his favorite thing to do. I talked about Chicago and my previous visits to London.

During the breaks, Don introduced me to other regular students, who made me feel just as welcomed. When Don took a break, Kyle danced with me while his buddy danced with his mom. I was enjoying myself more than I imagined and couldn't believe that over three hours ago, I had considered not coming at all.

By 11:30 p.m., the crowd's size had doubled as more people arrived. The dance party was in full swing. I said my goodbyes to everyone I met. Don and I added each other to our phones as Facebook friends before I descended the stairs, leaving the thumping bass behind.

Back on the street, shop signs and lights bounced off the slick wet pavement, leading back in the direction of the train. The quiet streets were empty, except for a few other people who were heading to catch the trains. The area felt safe with late-night cafes still open. I was not the least bit tired and was still reeling from the excitement of the night but knew with an early-morning departure, I should get at least a few hours of rest. Before heading back to the train, I grabbed takeout of chicken kabobs and fries from the Lebanese cafe across the street.

I was proud of myself; in a foreign place, I navigated an unfamiliar area on my own. The rain, jet lag, hesitation, and not having anyone to come with me hadn't stopped me from going out. I pushed aside my shyness and upped my determination to just have a good time. I was crossing over from a tourist to a traveler. I ventured out away from the hotel, away from the crew and overpriced tourist destinations. I got further outside of my comfort zone and learned to trust that despite being on my own, I would be safe. I was learning the art of choosing my own adventure.

WILL THEY REMEMBER WHEN AUNTIE TOOK THEM TO ITALY?

Tears glistened in her little brown eyes as my six-year-old niece looked up and asked me for the second time. "Auntie, will you spend the night with us?"

As if on cue, her twin brother chimed in and started begging.

"Puuuhleeeesseeee," he whined loudly, with instant tears streaming down his adorable chocolate face.

If I had not witnessed the mischievous yet adorable duo laughing hysterically at their own antics less than one minute before, perhaps I would have had a bit more sympathy. But, Auntie was worn out and had to get home to prepare for a trip in the morning. With the return of their parents, my babysitting duties were officially over. Like a good aunt, I kept them up past their bedtime and let them watch movies on a school night.

I think the tears were more about not being able to finish watching the *Despicable Me* movie rather than my departure.

Begging and crying was their best attempt at stalling the inevitable a bit longer.

"Okay, enough of the dramatics!" ordered my sister-in-law. "Give your aunt a hug and get in bed, now!"

My two munchkins lined up one after the other and tightly grabbed my waist as if hugging me for the last time ever. I stroked and kissed the top of their foreheads as they looked up at me. "I'll see you again soon. Be good, okay?"

They solemnly nodded as they clung to my waist.

Earlier that night, the three of us traveled to Italy by way of a fort in the living room made of sheets and blankets draped over the dining room chairs. Underneath the fort, piled with pillows and flashlights in hand, we searched their desk globe for the boot-shaped country.

"Look closer to Europe," I hinted.

"Victoria, scoot over. I think I know where it is."

"Ow, Damon! You're poking me in the arm! Stop!"

"Hey, hey! Stay focused on the goal, you two! Where is Italy?"

"I found Italy!" my niece yelled.

While in "Italy," we ate green Italian cookies before I presented them with the souvenirs I had bought for them in Venice last week. The twins screamed with excitement and thanked me for their gifts: a small copper-plated key chain in the shape of a pizza for my nephew and a beaded necklace with a little heart for my niece. I gave them branded pencils to add to their growing collection, which already included pencils from Dublin, London, Mexico City, and Barcelona. After I showed them photos of my trip to Italy, the three of us took turns telling spooky ghost stories with our flashlights aimed at our chins for dramatic visual effects.

Returning to our Naperville living room, we sat on the sofa and ate popcorn while watching the movie until their parents returned.

By the next week, I suspected the little necklace would be lost and my nephew will have probably traded his key chain for a cupcake. My hope, however, was that they would hang on to the memories and the excitement that comes with going to new places.

ESCAPE TO MEXICO

I stood at the top of the basement stairs and surveyed the damage. Broken pieces of ceiling lay strewn about Marsha and Miguel's basement floor, along with two inches of standing water. The carpet, the sofa, Miguel's workshop area, and the drafting table in the corner, along with stacks of books, photo albums, and old papers, were all soaked. Alternating between using a mop and a broom, Mike stood in the center, pushing puddles of water toward the floor drain.

"I came over to do my laundry and I heard water running," he said. "Walked down here and water was gushing from the ceiling."

Two hours ago, before I went over to their house, I texted Marsha on a below-freezing February evening to let them know I would be arriving to meet them in Puerto Vallarta, Mexico, within the next couple of days. I finally got the days off so I could join them for the third year in a row during their month-long winter vacation.

We're coming back tomorrow. Mike just texted us that a pipe burst in the basement. He's over there now, she replied.

Instead of packing to leave as planned that evening, I went over to help Mike clean up and salvage what we could. Far away from my mother's house in Atlanta, I considered Marsha and Miguel's home as my second home. When they were out of town and when I was between work assignments, I'd occasionally house-sit and watch TV in the basement until I fell asleep. They had become my adopted parents and I their adopted daughter. Mike kept an eye on the place as well, but apparently, none of us anticipated the unexpected and sudden deep-freeze. Retired and able to travel for long periods of time, Marsha and Miguel knew the only way to survive the winter version of Chicago was either to stay indoors or escape to a warmer climate.

I was going into my fourth winter as a flight attendant and my second one as a line holder. At every chance I could, as fall turned into winter, I picked up Orlando flights that no one really wanted. Most were either turns or two-day trips with short layovers.[15] For just a few hours of sunshine until I could get away for a longer occasion, I was willing to trap myself in a metal tube with hordes of unruly children and exhausted parents who were heading to and from Disney World. Each time, I vowed never again to work an Orlando flight before picking up another one the following week.

Now, at the height of winter, I was all set to join Marsha and Miguel for the third time on their annual winter vacation to Mexico. The past two years, I'd met up with them in Merida,

---

15 Turns are trips lasting one day and involve going to a destination and returning the same day.

Mexico. Located off the Gulf Coast of Mexico in Yucatan, I knew nothing about the place I was going other than it was warmer than Chicago and in good company. I was always thrilled to be invited. Plus, it was fun, navigating through unfamiliar cities by plane and buses to join them.

When I arrived in Merida, we stayed at an Airbnb. It was a spacious colonial townhome that was located near the bustling town center that had Spanish, French, and Mayan influences. During the day, the three of us explored the areas, sometimes revisiting the places Marsha and Miguel already had been before my arrival. I was instantly enamored with the vibrant city that had both a cosmopolitan feel and old-world charm. There were expansive city plazas, many flanked by towering Catholic cathedrals and historical museums. Along the pristine cobbled streets, Mayan women in traditional cotton dresses sat on the curbs underneath umbrellas with their children, selling their wares of baked goods, jewelry, and colorful hand-woven textiles. Throughout the day and late into the night in the plazas were festive dance performances and cultural plays adjacent to trendy European style patio cafes and restaurants where international and local tourists lounged. Music, along with the aromas of tortillas and slow-roasted meats from restaurants, filled the air and were carried along by a warm breeze. Until visiting Merida, I was only familiar with the overrun tourist party towns of Tijuana and Cancun, which held little interest for me. Exploring one of the oldest cities in the Americas, I began to discover Mexico as this huge, culturally diverse country with a rich history.

One of the many memorable moments in Merida was the day that Marsha and I went to the Mayan ruins of Dzibilchaltún, located less than an hour outside of Merida. She and Miguel already went earlier in the month and enjoyed it. It was my first time seeing such magnificent and ancient archaeological structures. Under the hot summer sun, Marsha took pictures of me from below as I carefully climbed the stone steps of the Temple of the Seven Dolls to survey the small city plaza of temples and stone structures. From above, I could see slow-moving iguanas crawling along grassy terrain and limestone pathways. After climbing down, Marsha and I sat and soaked our feet for hours in the famous freshwater *cenote* (pond) for a free fish pedicure. We alternated between giggles and yelps as the tiny fish tickled and painlessly nipped away at the dead skin on our feet.

My time with Miguel was equally treasured. When Marsha was tired or in relaxation mode, I'd go wandering around town with Miguel. We'd eventually end up finding a place to grab a beer before heading to the beach to watch the sunset.

Although born and raised in Mexico, Miguel lived most of his adult life in Chicago and was not always familiar with the places we visited. He was, however, more familiar with the food, customs, and language than Marsha and I. We often left it to Miguel to translate when needed or negotiate in Spanish the best prices for our souvenirs. I often asked him what foods I should try. I enjoyed spending one-on-one time with Miguel, wandering around town as I did with Marsha. Miguel always had interesting stories about his early life as a successful artist and I sometimes just liked listening to him talk. As with my own parents, I had a special relationship with each.

On another occasion, the three of us, along with Marsha's sister who had also come to visit, rented a car and drove to a nature preserve in the small fishing village of Celestun. At the nature preserve, we boarded a tiny motorboat driven by a local tour guide who led us through the Celestun River. After a few minutes on the boat, the narrow stream opened up into a massive lake that stretched for miles. Off in the distance, it appeared as if there was a thick layer of light pink foam covering the water, which would explain the water's reddish tint. As we got closer, I saw that the foam was actually a massive flock of startling cotton-candy-pink flamingos. Hundreds, if not thousands, of the swan-like birds with perfectly curved necks silently floated on the waters. Others stood on one razor-thin leg along the banks. As the motorboats approached, the flamingos sitting on the water quickly made way. They jumped to their feet into a full-out sprint. For less than five seconds, they ran on top of the water before taking flight. It was a magnificent and unforgettable sight!

One of the many things I found interesting about my travels with Marsha and Miguel is how they wandered around towns throughout Mexico separately and together. If one of them enjoyed a particular area in Mexico more, they would just plan to catch up with each other a few hours or a few days later. I admired the ease with which both of them, especially Marsha, moved about in new, unfamiliar places. Although Miguel was bilingual and Marsha spoke very little Spanish, she never relied on Miguel to be around as a translator. She was almost seventy (nearly the same age as my mother) and even shorter (about the same height too as my mother) than most Mexicans. Yet, she was just as comfortable navigating the tourist and local spots as if she lived there. Whenever it was just the two of us and we got turned around, which was often, she asked for directions in English or broken Spanish without hesitation. I, on the other hand, was not as nearly as confident using my Spanglish and was wary that vendors, knowing I was American, would try to sell me overpriced goods should I need help. I liked too that Marsha and Miguel were experienced travelers instead of tourists. They never stayed locked away at resorts or all-inclusive hotels. They enjoyed exploring as much as I did. They seemed to have spent a lifetime of leisure, traveling and visiting many of the places I wanted to go. It never bothered Marsha that Miguel talked for hours to local vendors as she and I browsed shops and local markets. After waiting a few minutes, Marsha and I would just wander away, leaving Miguel engrossed in a long conversation with his new best friend. Eventually we'd find him, sometimes in the same spot we returned to almost an hour later. I guess, having traveled for decades, they each knew and accepted one another's travel style.

Since Marsha and Miguel were no longer going to be in Puerto Vallarta, Mexico this year, I wasn't sure what to do with my short, five-day winter vacation. I was simply going because they were there.

"You should go anyways," suggested Marsha the next day when they returned home. I sat at the kitchen table with my hands resting on my chin as Marsha searched through stacks of papers, looking for the homeowner's insurance information. Miguel stood at the counter, preparing vegetables. Unless you opened the basement door, it would appear as though the home was unscathed.

"Is it safe?" I asked with a hesitant frown.

"The feeling of safety is relative," began Miguel philosophically. "Is Chicago safe?" he paused, pondering his own question.

"Can anyone say that anywhere is safe? What does it mean to be safe?"

I smiled as I always did in appreciation and amusement. Although a valid theoretical response, it was not the answer I was hoping for. Without losing focus on her task, Marsha's response was more reassuring.

"You'll be perfectly fine. Just don't wear expensive jewelry or make drug deals."

I was still doubtful.

"Plus, it's easy to get around on the little buses," she said. "There are different towns you can check out."

I was hesitant to go someplace new by myself where I didn't know anyone and especially in a non-English-speaking country. Sure, Dana and I had winged the unfamiliar territory of Costa

Rica without too many issues, but we were together. Between the two of us, we figured things out. If I were to travel alone for leisure, without friends or a crew who expected me to be back, at a certain time I'd have to figure out unfamiliar situations on my own. I wasn't too worried about being robbed as much as I was about being alone or getting lost in a foreign country. Yes, I was easily outgoing and confident in familiar surroundings when charged with a specific task. But, in unfamiliar places without a specific employment-related goal, I tended to be nervous and conservative. Traveling out of the country for the first time solo without reporting to a client or a company regarding my whereabouts would be outside my comfort zone.

That was the first indicator that I probably needed to go. If I was going to become the solo traveler I aspired to be, like the one I'd seen in magazines, powerfully standing on a mountain summit, overlooking some amazing valley view, I'd actually have to start traveling alone. I'd have to figure out where to stay and what to do on my own. Well, almost on my own – Marsha gave me recommendations on places to go and things to do. Miguel instructed me to try the shrimp burger when I got there although he couldn't remember the name of the restaurant.

When I booked my flight the following day from Chicago to Puerto Vallarta, I still wasn't thrilled about going solo. But, with my scheduled days off, I didn't have much to do and it was too cold to stick around. So, I said a prayer and headed out on the four-hour direct flight.

I spent my third and final evening thirty minutes away from the Puerto Vallarta airport in a sleepy little beach town called

Bucerías. It was one of the places Marsha recommended that she thought I would like, and of course, she was right. Bucerías was much quieter than the other larger beach towns that were overrun with tourists that I had visited over the past few days. Finally, I felt at ease walking through the town and along the spacious beach shore at sunset. The water and sand stretched for miles with only a handful of fellow beachgoers mostly keeping to themselves. In Bucerías, I didn't have to worry about the nonstop pestering of approaching vendors or navigating around clusters of beach chairs and umbrellas.

Reflecting on my trip, I slowly walked along the beach, enjoying the tickle of sand between my toes. I listened to the waves crash beneath the orange and purple sky. I think my first truly solo international trip was an overall success. It hadn't been filled with nonstop harrowing adventure, but I hadn't been killed, raped, or robbed in Mexico as I navigated from town to town along the Pacific west coast by bus. After spending a few days in downtown Puerto Vallarta, browsing shops and taking pictures of sculptures along the Malecón (boardwalk), I traveled up to a quirky, hipster town, Sayulita, where I sat and watched the surfers. Without too much trouble, I caught the local buses and easily found affordable yet basic accommodations in each place. I even got up the nerve to ask for help and directions when I needed them.

From time to time, I reluctantly bargained with vendors for souvenirs I really wanted, but I was pretty sure I didn't get the best price. Although I spoke some Spanish, I could never understand Mexican dialect. But fortunately, most understood what I was saying and almost everyone in the tourist districts spoke English. I spent my days sightseeing, exploring the shops, and checking out local food stands. In the evenings, after finding a place to stay, I'd find a restaurant near the water for dinner and wander the beaches until sunset. It definitely wasn't the same without Marsha and Miguel, but I could see why they enjoyed the place.

Sometimes, I chatted with a few locals and tourists, but I mainly stayed to myself. The towns were filled with retired Canadians and drunken American college students at night, stumbling and yelling from club to club along the boardwalks, where restaurants blared music and drink specials over loudspeakers.

In crowded areas, I kept an eye on my purse and frequently declined the vendors who were constantly trying to sell something as I passed by. "*La morena!*" they hollered and pointed at me to get my attention. "*De donde está?*" the men would ask. "Brown girl, where you from?" They were curious since I was usually the only Black person in all the towns I visited. Sometimes, if I felt up to it, I'd stop to have a conversation. Typically the men would try to sell me their wares or ask me out on a date; neither were of much interest to me. The local women and their tiny toddlers would often just stare at me quietly like I was a two-headed alien as I walked through the town. Children would gape and sometimes snicker. There was the occasional shouting and pointing of "*Ay! Negrita!*" to which I would give a self-conscious smile. Sometimes, I would frown, not understanding what else they were saying. It was unnerving because it sounded like another N-word, but I understood that I was just an unfamiliar sight. More so to them than they were to me.

In Bucerías, I was finally in a place where I felt as if I could relax. I was determined to get out of the comfort of my introverted shell and be more sociable. There had to be locals or even other tourists that I could relate to. When I met Carlos, I was walking along the beach at sunset by myself. He didn't impolitely stare or try to sell me something. In fact, before I met him, I met his two grayish-black dogs who haphazardly ran up to me. By now, I was used to everyone being curious and the approaching dogs did not faze me. Their wagging tales indicated they were enjoying the beach even more than me.

"Tutti! Fruitti! No!" a man's voice shouted above the waves. In the distance, I could see him trudge quickly through the sand, holding leashes and flip-flops in one hand. Although still a ways off, I could tell he was Mexican, a couple inches shorter than me, and wearing a t-shirt, beach shorts, and a well-worn baseball cap.

The dogs momentarily ceased sniffing at my feet to look up and debated whether or not to listen to the man calling for them. They playfully darted back to their owner.

"I sorry," he said as he approached with the dogs now circling him excitedly.

"No worries," I replied, letting each dog sniff my hand before petting them. "How old are they?" I asked, slowly pronouncing my words, unsure yet how well he knew English.

"They're one-year-old. Brother and sister."

I chuckled, recalling the names that he had shouted.

"Where are you from?" he asked. His English was pretty good.

"Chicago."

"Chee-cago. I've not been there yet, but want to go."

"Yeah, it's nice but cold right now. I like it here better."

"Me too. I walk with you. Yes?"

Used to saying "*No, gracias,*" I was getting ready to smile and politely decline before I remembered my personal goal. A few inches shorter than me and fairly scrawny, the friendly fellow beachgoer with slick dark hair underneath his baseball cap seemed harmless. If he wasn't, I could take him. Carlos and I continued a casual conversation as we walked along the beach. I got up the nerve to practice my Spanish. I was still cautious, but comfortable that he wasn't trying to sell me something. We walked for about an hour down the shore and back. Rather than going our separate ways, Carlos asked if I wanted to check out his place which was nearby. It was almost dark, but still early, and I didn't have any place to be. So I agreed.

Carlos and I sat side by side in two oversized hammocks on his rooftop, enjoying the gentle breeze coming from the ocean. We sipped tequila and watched twinkling lights on the other side of Banderas Bay. A banker from Mexico City, he had moved to Bucerías in search of a simpler life. He now sold high-end jewelry to well-off snowbirds and ran an imported vegan baked goods stand at the markets on weekends. He was learning to enjoy the good life, which I could appreciate.

"Your place is nice! The beach view is amazing," I commented.

"This place is ten thousand pesos a month," he said proudly.

That sounded like a lot of money. I pulled out my phone and entered the numbers into my currency converter. I entered the numbers to make sure the figure was correct.

Again, I got the same number.

Carlos was paying less than five hundred US dollars for a one-bedroom villa with a spacious rooftop terrace located less than a block from the beach! It was more than enough space for him and his two dogs, who had begun suspiciously eyeing me. Apparently, they liked me, but had not expected me to follow them home. The young duo sat underneath their owner's hammock, bored with our conversation, but alert should we decide to move.

Carlos and I talked for another couple minutes. Sometimes, we sat in silence. As he began drinking more tequila and getting chattier, I knew that was my cue to leave. Plus, I still hadn't bothered packing for my early-morning flight back. Only a few blocks from the cheap hotel I was staying at, I declined Carlos's invitation to walk me home. Although the streets were empty, they were well-lit. It was enough light to see the cobbled street ahead of me, yet still dark enough to admire the clear night sky, filled with twinkling stars.

The next morning, I left Bucerías and headed to the airport. I texted Carlos before I left to thank him for his hospitality and let him know that perhaps I would return sooner rather than later. I kept thinking about how getting a place of my own on the beach would be cheaper than renting an apartment with a roommate in Chicago. After studying abroad for six weeks, I'd always wanted to live in another country. Plus, it would give me a chance to practice my Spanish. I'd have to do some number crunching, but without being a millionaire, I could live near water. I could work, earn enough money within two or three weeks, and return each month to the beach.

My flight arrived back into Chicago in the late afternoon. Gazing out my window seat as the plane descended, it looked the same way as I had left it – cold and coated with snow and ice. An hour later, after going through customs and catching the train to Logan Square, I arrived back home with snot dripping from my nose from the cold. Exhausted, I lugged my bags up the front porch steps and then, once inside the front door, down again another flight of stairs to my basement room, as I always did. It felt like I had been gone for a month rather than a few days.

It also smelled like Brad hadn't taken a shower in a month. The small basement hallway was rank with his funk. After peeling off my coat and heading upstairs to use the bathroom, I ran into Debbie and discovered there was an additional roommate. While I was gone, Debbie had adopted a puppy as a playmate for Tux. A tiny Chihuahua more anxious than Tux sniffed at my feet before resuming his pursuit of the cat, who seemed to be enjoying it. Within a few hours, I'd soon discover that the puppy was not housebroken. After a few days of rest, I was eager to get back in the air, away from the smell of dried pee and small turds mixed with body odor.

Before heading out to work one morning, Debbie filled me in on a few more changes that happened while I was gone. In a couple of months, rather than renew the lease, she would be buying a home of her own. All of us would have to move or discuss a rent with the owner, who was more than likely going to sell the property to a developer. After more than three years in the same place, I felt as if it was time to move on. The rent for the basement room was ridiculously low even with the risk of flooding. Since I had been there, water seeped into the small basement room a couple of times during heavy rains. The only thing of importance that got wet was a pair of yoga pants I had left on the floor underneath the bed.

I was once again back to the drawing board with finding a place to live. This time, it wasn't as dire. Now that I had the schedule and flexibility, I could live anywhere in the world and commute to work by plane if I wanted to. I enjoyed Chicago, but my preference was someplace warm, near a beach, and affordable...

INTERNATIONAL HOUSE HUNTERS: BROKE FLIGHT ATTENDANT EDITION

I didn't tell too many people that I was moving to Mexico until my plans were final. Besides, before my first solo visit to Puerto Vallarta, my friends and family back in Atlanta were already overly concerned. I was still a bit unsure and knew that if I shared too many details of my plan, they could have easily talked me out of going.

"Is it safe?" my mother asked over the phone. Naturally, there was worry in her voice.

"It's fine, Ma," I assured her with the same phrase I'd repeated over and over to her since I was sixteen. Later in the same week, when I spoke to Maya, I could hear the doubt in her voice.

"Girl, you're going there by yourself? Watch out for the cartel – they are no joke!"

Maya had never visited Mexico and her knowledge of the cartel came from an *ABC News* special she and I had watched over a decade ago. True, at one point in time, I had those same concerns, but after visiting, I deduced that the entire country was not any more dangerous than the United States. I'd been zigzagging across the globe for a few years as a flight attendant, so you'd think they'd be used to me doing my own thing by now. But, I knew the thought of me moving to another country, even just on a part-time basis, was probably going to be too much for them to handle.

Like any place, I knew you had to be careful about going to certain areas and always keep an eye on your valuables. After talking with Marsha and Miguel and then visiting, I was confident I'd be safe living there on my own. Mexico was far from a violent, crime-riddled, lawless place, like in the movies and on the news. It was a media-fueled stereotype, and as a Black person, I knew all about those.

And if I didn't like it, I could always move back.

The next month, in between trips, I spent my time scouring the Internet, reading blogger sites and discussion forums, trying to get a sense of what it was really like to be a foreigner living in Mexico. My situation would be a bit different due to my job. I wasn't a retiree, digital nomad, or an ESL teacher. I wasn't going to be a Mexican resident or an expat – just a really frequent visitor. Along with searching the Internet, I sent a text to Carlos, who was my one and only contact there. He sent me a few links to check out. None were too helpful as they were in Spanish, which I could get the gist of, but not fully understand. Nevertheless, I appreciated the effort.

As I studied real estate and rental listings, most were targeted to visiting tourists; they were short-term and expensive vacation rentals. To really find a deal, I knew I'd have to get back there and do some old-fashioned boots-on-the-ground networking. I'd have to get to know someone who knew someone to get the beachfront hookup with Mexican rates. Sure, I didn't speak the language that well, but being brown instead of white may help rather than hurt my chances. It was ambitious I know, but if my hopes came true, I could have a nice place in sunny Mexico with enough income left over each month to rent a small room in Chicago to stay in between work trips. I did the math and my total expenses would still be cheaper than renting a one-bedroom apartment in a reasonably nice area of Chicago. Most importantly, I would have year-round access to sunshine. I was not rich enough to own multiple places throughout the world, but in the meantime, what I lacked in wealth I would make up for with creativity.

A few weeks before I decided to return to Mexico to begin looking, I emailed the owners of a bed and breakfast in Bucerías. Marsha mentioned in one of our conversations that she briefly met two American women who lived there during her last visit.

"I can't remember the name of their place. Gringo something," she said. "But, it had a cute little cafe and bookstore. It might be online. See if you can contact them." A quick Internet search pulled up Casa Tranquila and Gringo Bookstore.

I sent a quick email, inquiring:

To: Casa Tranquila
From: Nichole L. Davis
Date: February 2, 2016
Subject: Inquiry about Bucerías

I was recently in Bucerías and fell in love with the area. I'm thinking about relocating to the area for a few months and will be visiting again the first or second week in March to scout out the possibilities of a studio apartment within my budget for a move-in as early as late-March or the beginning of April. I'm a flight attendant with a flexible schedule, so it's easy for me to get back and forth. Do you have any rooms available in early-March and/or month-to-month rentals as early as April? Thanks for your time, I really appreciate it.

Nichole Davis

A month-and-a-half after my very first visit, I landed back at The Gustavo Díaz Ordaz International Airport in Puerto Vallarta. I could have taken a crowded minibus like I did the first time, but was tired and decided to splurge on an overpriced taxi to Bucerías. In stop-and-go traffic heading west along the Boulevard Francisco Medina Ascencio, everything along the way looked the same as I had left it. It was still a perfect 76 degrees with clear blue skies and sunshine. Towering palm trees lined the boulevard, accenting rows of upscale hotels and malls on each side. This time, I knew the point when the wide paved roads transitioned to a two-lane, dusty, dirty road as we moved farther away from the town's center. The vendors selling food in the middle of the street were still at the stoplights slowly wandering between cars displaying their goods of fresh-cut fruit, souvenir sombreros, and chicharrones. Although the beach wasn't in sight from the main road we traveled, I could smell the ocean breeze wafting through the taxi windows.

This time, I wasn't the least bit nervous. I was excited and focused. I'd already contacted several Airbnb owners, inquiring about possible places to rent long-term. I had a couple of appointments lined up. I was sure I could find more options once I hit the streets. I told Carlos that I was coming back to town and we made tentative plans to get together. He usually was busy when I texted him, but I hoped his schedule would allow him to check out a few places with me. I didn't want to rely on his help, but like with Miguel, if he was with me and would be willing to translate, I'd probably get a much better deal.

I arrived at Casa Tranquila right before dusk. It was located on a corner at the edge of the small town's tourist zone. Stepping out of the car, I caught a glimpse of the beach and waves crashing a block from Casa Tranquila. On my previous visit, I'd wandered along the beach town's main street, but didn't make it down the entire three-mile strip to the corner where Casa Tranquila intersected with the beginning of the beach. The property was hidden from the street by a high brick wall draped with flowering greenery. A sign hung above the small black wrought-iron gate door, letting me know I was at the right place. The area, rustic and charming like the rest of the town, was slightly more commercial. It was the center of action and the primary access to the water.

A petite older white woman with bright blue eyes opened the gate to greet me as the taxi drove away. She was comfortably dressed in an embroidered Mexican housedress. I recognized her immediately from the website picture as one of the two owners. She looked the same, except her curly gray hair was now mostly white with a purplish rinse that matched the colors in her dress.

"Nichole? Welcome! Hi, come on in. I'm Patricia!" For the past few weeks, I'd been corresponding by email with Patricia. Her emails, warm and friendly, matched her in-person demeanor.

Patricia led me to the patio where a handful of hotel guests lounged at the cafe tables in a tropical courtyard with plants and flowers everywhere. Casa Tranquila was aptly named. It is a private, shaded oasis in the center of the dusty beach town. Standing in the center of the courtyard, a small two-story set of bungalow apartments were to my left, and on the opposite end of the courtyard to my right was a patio, leading to the inside of a small bookstore. A few feet away, partially obscured by towering palms and more flowers, was a pool with a large inflatable flamingo floating on the bright turquoise water. Butterfly and bird mobiles dangled from small flowering trees all around the area.

"Your room's almost ready. We're setting up the bed. Get comfy," encouraged Patricia, motioning me to the chaise lounge, draped with a handcrafted Mexican throw blanket. I happily obliged.

In her email, Patricia mentioned that the rooms were full except for the Betty Boop room that was named after Patricia's mother Betty, who frequently stayed in the small guest room that doubled as the property's massage room. It was affordably priced and available for the few days I needed, which Patricia informed me was during the high season. This was a good sign. Most of the places I investigated as my "headquarters" were full. The few properties available ranged from a couple of hundred to over a thousand dollars per night.

The screen door of one of the bottom bungalow apartments opened and Joanne, the other owner I recognized from the website, stepped out. Slightly taller than Patricia and around the same age in her sixties, Joanne wore thin wire-rimmed glasses and a vibrant smile. She greeted me with a warm hug as the two kittens scampered between her and over my feet before quickly catapulting into a nearby tree.

"And that's Dude and Ninja," she said.

Once again, I had the feeling of being at home away from home.

That evening, after I got settled in, Joanne and Patricia invited me to join them for dinner on the patio. They showed me a map of the town and areas where I should look for rentals. They were familiar with many of the people I was scheduled to meet with and also referred me to additional property owners to contact.

"The low season is starting soon, so you should be able to find something decent," said Patricia. "Unless you're looking for one of the fancy condos they threw up yesterday, which I wouldn't recommend."

"Yeah, like all things, this town is changing," said Joanne.

Although still quaint, Bucerías, known as a small fishing village, was rapidly transforming from a hidden gem to a burgeoning tourist destination. The town had yet to be flooded with the pricey high-rise condos that overran Puerto Vallarta and its overflow city Nuevo Vallarta, but within a few years' time, it was inevitable. During my previous visit, I had noticed several construction sites that seemed oddly out of place between the one-story shops and restaurants.

Joanne and Patricia were best friends who had lived in various parts of Mexico for more than thirty years. In 1991, they decided to leave their hometown in Anchorage, Alaska, and drove in the '64 VW Micros from Alaska to Mexico in search of a warmer climate. They arrived in Puerto Vallarta, Mexico, and eventually became Mexican citizens. They bought land and owned several businesses. During their lifetimes, they had traveled all around the world and now hosted friends from everywhere, many of whom came to visit annually. Mexico had become their home and they were a loved part of the community. It was an honor to be welcomed into their international family of travelers, and their bold spirit for adventure inspired me.

On my first night back in Bucerías, Joanne and Patricia had gone above and beyond being helpful. My heart was filled with such gratitude for the two as I navigated a new place that I wanted to call home. Any lingering doubts I had about my decision were gone. I was in good company of world travelers that saw nothing odd or unusual about packing up and moving across a border. I would be more than okay. Living a life filled with new adventure, peace, and the beach was not a someday dream or something that I'd have to do when I retired or got rich. It was a near-future reality that was off to a good start as another goal achieved.

The next day, after a comfortable sleep in Betty Boop, I got up and out after a cup of coffee on the cafe patio. Since my first showing wasn't until the afternoon, I wandered around town, revisiting the favorite beach spots and restaurants from my first trip. It was early in the morning and fewer people were around than in the previous month. I had purposely planned to return in March, as the high season was winding down in the area and vacancies were expected in April. This meant more landlords were willing to lower their rates to have their places occupied.

On my third and final full day in Bucerías, I had asked around and toured several possible places I could rent. They were far from ideal and none were thrilling, although most were within my small budget. There weren't any hammocks, ocean views, or anywhere close to being as spacious and private as Carlos' place. In fact, when I arrived in Puerto Vallarta, I didn't hear much from Carlos. He was busy at markets outside of town and unavailable. I was on my own looking at places, but I was determined not to get discouraged since I also had help from Joanne and Patricia. Had space been available, I would have easily rented an extended place from them. Understandably, all their spaces had been booked a year in advance.

My first option was a tiny first-level studio on a side street. It was close to the beach, but not on it. The view right outside the door was a cement wall with white chipping paint on the opposite side of the narrow street. Although a block from the beach, the room looked more like a dark broom closet rather than a room. The current occupant, a heavy smoker, planned to vacate by April. The idea of having my very own smoke-filled closet near a beach was not that appealing. The second was a long-term apartment unit. It was located right in the center of town, a couple of doors down from Casa Tranquila, but it wasn't the same vibe at all. The room was above a storefront that appeared to be under renovation.

"It's steps away to the beach," said the property manager as he led me around bags of cement, work tools, and bricks that littered the property.

The room, consisting of a bed, TV, microwave, and nightstand, was unimpressive. The view from the balcony to the beach was more than partially obstructed by a nearby building, along with electrical wires that I could reach out and touch. Should I choose either place, my refuge would simply have to be the beach and definitely not my living quarters.

I saw several other less-attractive places, even farther from the beach and smaller. I didn't consider the other room on the second floor of the building that not only was unfurnished but was also absent of a balcony railing on the entire second-floor walkway. Although the room was within my budget, one misstep on a dark night would lead me to landing on the first floor with a broken leg. My second-worst choice was a spacious yet dim house. The three other bedrooms were closed and locked. The owner (or rather, the man who claimed to be the owner) allowed me to tour the kitchen and assured me that the room was nice and could be ready by my desired move-in date.

I returned to Casa Tranquila to assess my options, followed by a nap. I wrote the pros and cons of my top two choices. I'd need to make a decision and leave a deposit before I left the following day. I was not thrilled with either prospect, but at least I would have a place to stay and could always look for better options once I was settled in Mexico.

In the evening, I joined Patricia, Joanne, and one of their friends, Sarah, for dinner at Aduato's Restaurant on the beach. Sarah was a retired Canadian snowbird who had been spending winters in Bucerías for the past six years. With the winter winding down, she was heading back to Canada later that week eager to spend time with her daughter and new grandchild.

"If you want, you can check out my place," she said over dinner. "It's on the other side of the highway though."

The highway, MEX-200, was a four-lane boulevard leading in and out of Bucerías. The side of the highway where I'd spent my last few days looking was closest to the beach and considered the tourist district where many retirees lived due to its easy access to the outdoor restaurants, shops, and bars. On the other side of the highway, up in the hills, were neighborhoods where most Mexican residents of Bucerías lived. I really wanted something within walking distance from the beach, somewhat familiar, and doubted that Sarah's place would be a fit. But, with two less-than-stellar options, I was willing to keep an open mind at other possibilities. I agreed to see her place and we made arrangements for me to come by in the morning before I headed to the airport.

The next morning, Patricia and Joanne gave me walking directions to Sarah's house. Taking a shortcut, it was less than ten minutes away from Casa Tranquila and right on the other side of the highway. Her place was not even a five-minute walk to a beach access point away from the busy central area. As I followed the instructions to find her place, I took note of surrounding homes in her neighborhood. It was starkly different from the cute, flower-covered high- and low-rise buildings on the other side of the street. The homes along the cobbled street were typical of a working-class rural neighborhood. The nondescript houses were basic, cement, painted structures of various colors crammed side by side, each with small windows and wooden front doors. It was a neighborhood, nevertheless, that was far from desolate, with children laughing and playing in front of their houses as older adults and seniors sitting outside their home. On the corner of the block where Sarah lived was a small bodega, and across the street was an open-air barbershop.

On the opposite side of the corner from the barbershop, tucked between two homes, was a narrow alley with vibrant red-bricked walkway that led to Sarah's place. The alleyway walls were painted orange and large potted plants and flowers lined the path. I turned the corner and stepped into a spacious courtyard, hidden from street view. It was as if I had walked into a remixed version of Casa Tranquila. Sunlight flooded the courtyard patio garden that doubled as a front entrance to

Sarah's ranch home. The space was covered with roses and lush greenery; the centerpiece of the courtyard was a stone fountain, spouting water. Surprised by its beauty, I quietly followed Sarah up the stairs and into her home. It was a compact, brick ranch home that was hidden away on an incline and looked nothing like the simple surrounding homes of neighbors.

"I bought this from an American who gutted and renovated the existing home," she explained. "They added the Mexican tiles to the tub and all throughout the kitchen."

She toured me through the home as I admired the Mexican artwork that hung along the living room walls. It was a two-bedroom, one and a half bath home with more space than I needed. Instead of a beach view out my front window, I would have an amazing garden view. I was more than willing to settle. Sarah, needing someone to watch over the place while she was away, made the rent affordable. I now had a place of my own (for six months anyway) in Mexico!

My scouting mission was beyond the success I had imagined. I was hopeful, but hadn't expected to find the amazing place that I had envisioned in my head. With a location now secured, I returned to Chicago to pack up my small room and move out. With a place of my own – two blocks from the beach in Mexico – I now just had to find a tiny space in Chicago to crash between trips.

LIFE IN EL BARRIO

Adjusting to life in Mexico was an easier transition than moving to Chicago – I knew a few people already, I had a place to stay, and most importantly it wasn't cold when I moved in. A few days before Sarah returned to Canada, she introduced me to her neighbors, including José, her gardener who lived next door, and Juanita, the housekeeper who lived across the street. José would tend to the garden and Juanita would clean the house before I arrived each month and after I departed. Although living alone as a foreigner in another country, in an unfamiliar neighborhood, where everyone knew that I lived alone, I felt safe, especially since I now knew people nearby.

Every month for a week, sometimes two weeks when I could, I returned to Mexico after I finished all my trips. My daily routine when I first arrived frequently consisted of morning workouts and afternoons working on writing projects.

In the evenings, I strolled along the beach before sunset and picked up tacos from the corner stand before heading back home. Eventually, I put up a hammock in the courtyard patio, and, when not writing, I spent my afternoons lounging in the hammock or playing music.

It took getting used to having so many neighbors and seeing them every time I walked out the door. Everyone was friendly and would say hello. Having forgotten most of my Spanish, I was often nervous to engage in too much small talk. The most patient of my neighbors who understood the most English was Juanita, who would frequently come by a day or two after my monthly arrival with Dulce, her curious eleven-year-old daughter, in tow. Upon first meeting me, her daughter, a chubby young girl with dark cinnamon-colored cheeks and bright eyes, exclaimed excitedly to her mother, "*Ella es morena como yo!*" She's brown like me!

Juanita and I eventually became friends and so too did Dulce and I. In the evenings, Juanita and I would sit outside on the street with the other neighbors and talk. Between my Spanglish and hand gestures, we understood each other well. When not playing with the other neighborhood kids, Dulce, who understood less English than her mother, would be at her side, telling me about her day in rapid-fire Spanish. I would smile with delight and furrow my eyebrows, only getting a gist or two. In Spanish, her mother would encourage the chatty young girl to slow down so I could understand.

My most amusing and sporadic visitor however, was a four-year-old boy named Omar who I met a few days after my arrival. I was writing in the living room, and upon hearing a rustling outside, I looked out my large front window to see a small boy open the entrance gate I left unlocked during the day. Rather than walking to the front door, he played in the fountain and made himself right at home. Perplexed, but not minding the company, I quietly watched the little boy play in the water and wander around the garden for a few minutes before I went to the front door.

"Hola," I smiled. He smiled back and walked up the stairs as if I was expecting him. I realized that perhaps he was the only person in the neighborhood that did not know of Sarah's departure.

"¿Estás buscando Sarah?" *Are you looking for Sarah?* He solemnly nodded.

"Sarah no está aqui." Disappointment registered across his face. I suddenly remembered seeing a small stash of Coca-Cola bottles and chocolates in the refrigerator that Sarah left behind. I offered the boy a soda and he walked right in. His big brown eyes beamed as he gave me a crooked smile. Omar climbed onto the kitchen counter stool as I went into the refrigerator to retrieve his soda and candy. Ten minutes later, a woman called Omar's name from the gate. Omar climbed down and waved bye as he headed out the door. I waved to his mom as she apologized.

"*No es problemo*," I said laughing. "*Hasta luego Omar.*"

As high season died down and the rainy season began, my excitement of living in Mexico dipped. I still enjoyed it, but the heat and humidity often forced me out of the un-air-conditioned house during the day. Unable to concentrate on writing, I'd go over to visit with Patricia and Joanne at Casa Tranquila for late-morning coffee and cool off in the shade while playing with the kittens. Between their work and tending to their guests, I'd chat with Joanne, Patricia, and the staff or browse through the bookstore. The gringo cafe was a social spot for guests and expats, many of whom were retirees.

Throughout the year-and-a-half that I lived in Mexico and commuted to Chicago for work, a handful of friends from the states also came to visit at different times. We'd go do all the tourist stuff that I normally didn't do, which included whale-watching, hiking, and kayaking. We'd lounge on the beach and I'd take them to visit my favorite places again as if I'd never been. At night, depending on our mood, we'd go out to dinner and late-night clubs in Puerto Vallarta.

When I didn't have friends in town, I'd go visit Lisa, who lived an hour away by bus in the Conchas Chinas neighborhood located south of Puerto Vallarta. Lisa and I met during a group hike I found on one of the local Facebook activities group pages. A quirky and sincere red-headed Canadian expat around my age, Lisa and I quickly became friends over our shared love of hip-hop music and an appreciation of Mexican artists. Having moved from Canada with her mother several years earlier, the two of them rented a traditional Mexican ranch villa nestled in a rocky cove of the exclusive lower section of the Amapas neighborhood. When not out exploring the city, she and I would sit on the eclectic patio, which was overflowing with lush plants, crystals, and wind chimes. We'd sit for hours watching the waves calmly and melodically crash against the rocks fewer than fifty feet from the porch. Eating Mexican takeout that was delivered from a nearby restaurant and listening to her well-curated collection of hip-hop and house beats, we'd relish our charmed life in Mexico.

Despite the handful of close friends and welcomed guests, I had my fair share of mortal enemies that made Mexico less than perfect. Although most of the neighbors I met were cool, the rooster that lived next door was not. In fact, we never officially met, but at 4 a.m., the first night I was in my new place, I could hear it. Until that moment, I always thought that roosters crowed at sunrise. I'm not sure if it was a regional thing, but in Mexico, they did not crow. They screeched, and it happened waaaay before sunrise and all the way into the late afternoon. Separated from the neighboring homes due to the slight elevation and high walls, I never saw this rooster, but could always – and I mean always – hear it.

During my first week after I moved in, I didn't sleep for more than a few hours at night. I tried earplugs and then playing music through my headphones. Neither drowned out the rooster, perched out of view somewhere above my bedroom skylight. For days, after I was startled awake in the middle of the night and unable to go back to sleep, I fantasized about different ways to kill a rooster. In desperation, I spent way too much money on a pair of noise-canceling headphones. When I played an endless loop of airplane engine white noise with the volume set to high, I could finally drown out the rooster and sleep through the night.

Although a nuisance, the rooster was not the biggest threat to my way of life in Mexico. The next unwelcomed visitor proved to be a more formidable foe. I was watching Netflix on the couch one evening in the dimly-lit living room when, out of the corner of my eye, I saw something move. At first, I thought it was the light coming from the computer screen, but I glanced up to see something up in the corner between the wall and the ceiling that hadn't been there before. From a distance, it looked like a thick black dust ball or a newly installed security camera. As I got up to get a closer look, I froze in disbelief. The "dust ball" was the diameter of a tennis ball with furry legs and beady eyes staring directly at me. For the first time ever, I was face to face with a wolf spider.

Although terrified, I knew that I had to act quickly. Without breathing or taking my eyes from the spider, I quietly backed away to get the can of Raid from the kitchen sink. Holding my breath, I crept once again toward the spider with my finger firmly on the nozzle. Stretching my arm upright, I aimed and started shooting. I screamed and leaped back as the spider jumped from the corner and lunged toward me. Without lifting my finger from the nozzle, I kept spraying my target without mercy. The spider landed on the tiled floor and sprinted a few inches away, attempting to escape. A second later, as my liquid assault continued, the monster's sprint turned to a jog and finally, a desperate crawl, before coming to a complete stop. I kept spraying for good measure until it curled itself into a ball. The full can was now halfway empty. When I was 200 percent certain it was dead, I stopped spraying. The entire house smelled like Raid and my eyes were stinging. Without remorse, I murdered the biggest spider I'd ever seen in my life.

A few nights later, I was once again sitting in the living room with all the lights on. I watched as another large spider crawled right underneath my front door onto the living room floor. Instinctively, I snatched the Raid from the side table and leaped into action. Sensing my determination and its imminent death, the spider turned around and scurried right back from where it came. A braver, more fearless version of me sat the can of Raid back on the table, returned to the couch, and continued my Netflix binge.

Six months later, when Sarah returned, I moved into a smaller place that I had once again found through networking. Through a ladies group on Meetup, I had met a few cool middle-aged women who invited me to join them for a poolside lunch on random afternoons. One of the women I met was Carol. Carol, like Sarah, was also from Canada. Carol and her husband owned several properties in Bucerías. While most of their properties were luxury condos well out of my price range, she mentioned that in the back of their home was a casita available to rent.

The one-bedroom room casita, although small, was unbelievably priced at $150 a month. It was the size of a pool house, tucked a few feet away from the main residence which was a large two-story villa. The high palapa roof was made of thatch that, although it helped with ventilation, it required constant sweeping of dust and small fallen leaves off of the floor and furniture. The casita's front entrance was a panel of glass that opened out to a beautiful garden of massive palms that separated the main house from the casita. A marble writing desk that doubled as a small dining table looked directly out the entrance into the garden. In the bedroom, which contained a twin bed, wardrobe closet, shower, and toilet, there was a back door, leading out into the dusty, unpaved back alley that served as my private entrance. The tiny casita was well-maintained, with exactly enough space for one person.

The price was perfect. My first six months of moving and living in Bucerías had been more expensive than I projected. I needed to cut back on my spending considerably if I was to continue going back and forth. There was still a lot more I wanted to see and do in Mexico.

My new neighborhood was rather far from the town center and beach. It was a 15-minute walk to the beach and a short bus ride to the center of town. The area consisted of newly constructed houses built by Americans and Canadians of modest means. The homes, each hidden by high walls, were all clustered together on individual plots of land. There weren't any Mexican neighbors sitting on their porch or children playing. I never saw familiar faces when I walked out the door. There was little traffic along the dusty streets that had yet to be paved. Stray dogs and chickens roamed near piles of trash and discarded brush from nearby fields. Down the street from the home, off the main road, was a construction staging area where large, frequently used semi-trucks lined the street. My new area was not quite as picturesque as my previous one, but I was still content.

Despite the change in location, I still had a few welcomed and unwelcomed visitors. The parade of critters in and out of the casita included an iguana that stayed hidden in the thatched palapa roof. Occasionally, I would hear a rustling above my head or see its tail hanging on the wall where the ceiling and the roof met. I figured as long as it stayed hidden in rooftops and quiet at night, we wouldn't have any problems. While I no longer had children visiting, my favorite daily visitor was Cleo, one of Carol's three guard dogs that roamed the property. Although the other two dogs paid me very little attention, Cleo paid me too much attention. Whenever I was standing at the tiny stove in the casita cooking, she would sniff around under my feet, waiting for food to accidentally drop on the floor. During the rainy-season nighttime thunderstorms, Cleo pawed at the closed casita door until I let her inside. She and I kept each other company, waiting for the rain to pass.

As someone who enjoyed privacy and quiet times in Mexico, it was sometimes uncomfortable living with my landlords on-site. Often, when I stepped into the garden, Carol, her husband, or gardeners would be out in the garden, either lounging or working. Although I sometimes enjoyed chit-chatting, I was often drained from just getting back into town or working on writing projects. I had to be mindful of not playing music or talking on the phone too loudly. Since I could hear conversations and noises coming from the main house as if I had roommates, I was sure that they could hear mine. The casita was not as secluded or private as I would have enjoyed, but for the price, I was still okay for the time being.

CAFÉ, TÉ, O YO? (COFFEE, TEA OR ME?) PART II

As far as the possibility of a romantic relationship, a part of me expected my dating life to improve the instant I arrived in Mexico. My energy and excitement would automatically attract the man of my dreams. As I wandered around town, I imagined he'd spot me perusing the little artisan shops. After seeing me sitting alone a couple of times in the town's restaurant and cafes, he'd finally get up the nerve to introduce himself. Perhaps, he'd be a globetrotter too, seeking a travel partner, or he'd be a local, independently wealthy musician who could teach me how to salsa.

I even thought perhaps Carlos and I would get to know each other better. Eventually, I wouldn't mind that he was significantly shorter than me. I didn't see Carlos at all during my scouting trip. However, a few weeks after settling into Sarah's place, I eventually ran into him again on the beach. His response was short yet polite as he was getting ready to walk by without stopping, almost as if he didn't recognize me. How many women had been on this man's rooftop hammock?

"How are you doing?" I asked, hesitant.

"I good and you? You find a place?"

He knew who I was.

"I did. I live on the other side of the highway."

"Good, good. I see you around? Yes."

"Sure, take care."

I wondered if Carlos's aloofness had something to do with me politely refusing his advances the night we met. But soon, I realized that it probably had more to do with another female tourist that I noticed by his side a few days later. A middle-aged white woman with black and gray hair, they appeared to be a couple. In that instance, he glanced in my direction and then quickly looked away. I wasn't too disappointed; I was making other friends and knew it would be only a matter of time before I was strolling alongside the beach, holding hands with someone too.

Meeting people in Mexico was easy, but I soon learned dating in Mexico was a bit trickier. Bucerías was a forty-minute drive from downtown, and my little town was mostly filled with vacationing families and retirees. On the few nights I went into town, the clubs were filled with young, drunk affluent bro-like guys, which were not really my type. As a semi-resident, I quickly learned to stay away from the tourist spots. The local bars weren't much better. No one spoke much English and I didn't speak enough Spanish. As the only Black person, I would get stares of curiosity from both men and women. Occasionally, I would get propositioned from local men, assuming I was a tourist. I had zero interest in such arrangements. Since I didn't surf, do drugs, or drink alcohol until I blacked out, I soon realized that my prospects for meeting someone compatible in the typical Mexican social settings were going to be few and far in between.

After a while, I did go on a few first dates, but rarely second ones. I met a several guys from Tinder who were cool and interesting, yet there wasn't the chemistry that I hoped for. I wasn't going to be with someone simply for the sake of not being lonely - I'd done that in my twenties. But, among the handful of dates, there were occasions where I began to think maybe a fling wouldn't be so bad. The Chilean skydiver that lived for his next jump could be a contender, or even the Hungarian backpacker that was passing through Mexico after his time in Peru. In the end though, I figured, my version of *Eat, Pray, Love*[16] would come together if I just gave it more time. Besides, as a frequent visitor to the taco stall at the end of the block where I lived, I had already nailed the eating part.

---

16 A bestselling book and movie about a woman traveling the world to discover her true self.

BLOG POST:
IT'S VALENTINE'S DAY SO WHAT?

Chi Mc Fly | April 12, 2018 | Released to Crew Rest

N o one has asked and no one cares what I'm doing for Valentine's Day. It's all good, though.

My only plans are to catch a flight back to Chicago for work after spending two long weeks in Mexico. There's neither a Mexican bae for a beach Valentine's Day breakfast before I leave nor a Chicago bae, greeting me with flowers at the airport when I land.

Many who learn about my lifestyle of travel and leisure assume that I come to Mexico so frequently because I have someone here. The Mexican men assume that since I'm walking around alone, I probably have someone back home. If not, they inquire if I'm looking for a "Mexican Romeo," aka tourism sex.

Nope and nada nope.

I'm single as a dollar bill – kind of on purpose and kind of by default of my travel lifestyle. I'm solo for the time being and that's okay.

I must admit, as I'm getting older being alone is wearing on me a bit. I want someone to rub my feet when I get off work. A few romantic getaways would be ideal. No matter how lonely I get, I refuse to settle for anything less than real.

So in the meantime, I'll continue to wander the world solo or with good friends.

"Why aren't you married? Why don't you have kids?"

I'll keep shrugging my shoulders because neither are simple answers. The short answer is that I'm too busy enjoying life.

The long answer has to do with the shady guys (or just plain boring ones) I attract these days. Maybe I'm just picky. No, my friends would say that I'm not picky, just selective.

But, I can't be at all bitter or sad for too long because there's the beach, beautiful sunsets, and so many new places to explore...

I'LL TAKE COFFEE NOW!

Traveling from Mexico to Chicago and Chicago to Mexico every month became my new norm and I liked it. I enjoyed border-hopping, going from hot to cold then back to the hot. Working on the plane was joyful because I knew that as soon as I was done, I'd be heading back to sunshine and sand. Cranky passengers, weather delays, and schlepping luggage through terminals was simply a means to an end.

My end was always Puerto Vallarta.

My small corner in Chicago was as comfortable as I needed it to be. The following month after I moved my few belongings to Mexico and left the rest in storage at my friend Irma's place, I surprisingly found a perfectly priced room without much effort. I posted an ad on good 'ole Craigslist about needing a place to crash between trips and within a matter of weeks, I found a small room in Logan Square. It was not too much more than what I was previously paid in Debbie's basement and fortunately with fewer roommates. My landlord Violet was a recent divorcee and French grad student looking to sublease the rooms of her three-bedroom brownstone next to the L stop. Furnished with a bed, small table, and blackout curtains, it was a convenient and comfortable space to rest for a day or two between trips. In class or working, I rarely saw Violet, and she had yet to find a third roommate, so the place was always quiet.

From the outside looking in, it would seem as though my constant travels were chaotic. In one moment, I'm in Mexico. In the next, I'm in Chicago and then Florida, followed by flights to Baltimore and Seattle – all within three days. Yet, despite being on the go, constantly packing and repacking with little downtime in between, there was a continuity and stability that I hadn't had in years. Weather delays during work trips were my only source of unpredictability, which no longer bothered me.

My writing business was picking up, too. I started working on more book projects and participated in small-business retreats in Morocco and Paris. Even though I was still casually dating now and then, having a boyfriend fell low on the list of priorities. And then, I met Max.

It was still dark outside at 4:34 a.m. when I dragged myself, and my luggage through the hotel lobby to the awaiting crew shuttle van that was scheduled for departure in one minute. The driver stood at the back of the vehicle, waiting for my arrival so we could go. Seeing the look of exhaustion on my face, he gave me a sympathetic good morning nod as I approached and handed him my luggage to load.

"Morning," I muttered to everyone while climbing into the van. I was unbothered by my almost-late arrival. I made it in time and that's really what mattered. During the seven-minute drive from the hotel to the Miami-Dade airport, the various crews from different airlines sat in silence, mentally preparing for the brutally long day ahead of us. I wasn't the only one operating on minimum crew rest[17].

After entering the departures terminal, filled with weekday business travelers, I began scanning the area for the nearest Starbucks. I was barely keeping up with the herd of flight crew who were all walking in the same direction to the employee security checkpoint. My crew had fifteen minutes before we were scheduled to be at the gate and I desperately needed my morning caffeine fix. As I stood in the security line, waiting on my turn for the conveyor belt, I noticed for the first time that morning an unfamiliar face among my Newark-bound crew. He was a tall, older man (maybe about fifty) with a bald head, tanned olive skin, and a thick yet neatly trimmed mustache. He politely gestured for me to go ahead of him in line.

"Hey, how are you this morning?" he said cheerfully, with a clipped accent as he extended his hand to greet me. "I'm Max. I think I'm working up in the front galley with you to Newark."

Max was the chaser for the first of three segments for the day. [18] His freshly pressed uniform, along with the mustache and cheerfulness, gave me the impression that he was gay, which of course was not uncommon since the majority of male flight

---

17 The minimum amount of time flight attendants are required to have by federal law between duty days is about 8 hours from landing to departure. Depending on the time it takes to unload passengers, walk through the terminal, wait for the shuttle, check-in to hotel and shuttle back, we're lucky if we get six hours of actual sleep.

18 Chaser, also known as the extra crew, is usually an additional crew member added onto one or more flight segments in order to meet the minimum staffing requirements for a flight. This flight attendant usually works with different crews throughout their scheduled assignment that can last one or more days.

attendants are gay. But, I thought to myself, at second glance, he could just be European and still straight, which would explain his chivalrous behavior and subtle but not offensive pretentiousness. Plus, having dated several European men, I found them to be absent of hyper-masculinity and more expressive in general. I shook his hand after allowing him to help me heave my luggage onto the conveyor belt for scanning.

"I'm Nichole," I quickly replied as we followed our belongings down the line. I was puzzled by his formality, which is usually displayed by overeager pilots who want their breakfast served to them before takeoff. As we continued down the line, awaiting our belongings to come through on the other side, Max followed closely behind me, attempting to engage in typical first-time coworker small talk. Such chitchat was usually appropriate, but not at such an ungodly hour.

"Where did you all come in from last night?"

"Chicago."

"I came in from LA. I'm scheduled for Charlotte after this segment."

I didn't respond. It took all the focus I could muster to put my bags on the security conveyor belt, let alone pay attention to what he was talking about. Quickly grabbing my belongings from the other side of the belt, I allowed my thoughts to drift back to finding coffee. Max either did not notice or care that the other two members of our crew were not yet awake or talking much to him either. Since he'd be working in the front galley with me, I tried my best to be polite and forced a quick smile.

"I'm going to get coffee. I'll meet you at the gate," I informed the crew as they continued gathering their belongings from the conveyor belt.

With two minutes to spare before our official report time at the gate and ten minutes before boarding, I made my way down the jet bridge with my Starbucks coffee in hand. Max stood at the aircraft door with his arms relaxed behind his back as if I were the first passenger to arrive. He opened the small closet door to help me stow my luggage away. Had my coffee kicked in, perhaps I would have found his courteous manner thoughtful, but it hadn't.

This guy is doing too much. I hope it's not going to be like this for the whole flight.

During boarding, as I sorted through the galley and prepped the first-class meals, I listened as Max enthusiastically and sincerely greeted the incoming passengers. My mood lightened and my pace quickened as the coffee pulsed through my veins.

"Max, where are you from?" I asked, hoping he didn't take offense to my curt responses earlier.

"A little bit from everywhere. I was born in Australia, raised in Germany, and spent a bit of my life in Japan as well."

"Oh, that's interesting," I said and meant it. Having been to Germany and with Japan and Australia on my bucket list, I was looking forward to hearing more about Max's travels.

During the intermittent breaks in boarding, I learned that Max was based in Los Angeles and started working with the airlines six months ago. Although hired as a Dutch speaker, he, like other international reserves, were frequently drafted to work on domestic flights when needed. He was a shiny new hire and an international flight attendant, which explained his enthusiasm and most of his awkwardness. After a few more minutes as we prepared the plane for 6 a.m. takeoff, I felt compelled to match his friendliness. Although initially annoying, his enthusiasm became contagious.

Following takeoff to cruising altitude, Max and I sat shoulder to shoulder on the jump seat.

"What did you do before?"

It was my favorite question to ask all new flight attendants.

"I was an engineer, but it wasn't what I was meant to do," he thoughtfully replied.

His response surprised and intrigued me. "What do you mean?"

"Well, being of service and contributing to others has always been important to me. Engineering paid well, but it wasn't fulfilling."

"So, you became a flight attendant?"

For the next hour as we served passengers, Max and I chit-chatted in the galley about our experiences. He was ten years older than me and seemed to have had several lives as an engineer, a hospice worker, and at one point in time, a shamanic healer in Peru, which I would have never guessed. As he spoke about some of the people who inspired him, I began to admire the depth of his caring and concern for others. We passionately talked about our travels, our commitment to self-discovery, and our spiritual paths. We were both fascinated by each other's life journeys that led us to work for the company that gave us unlimited access to the world. Such conversations with other flight attendants were out of the ordinary. Max and I, however, were kindred spirits.

It was 8 a.m. Eastern time when we landed in Newark. I was energized and excited by having such an enjoyable flight and intellectually stimulating discussion. Before we landed, Max and I exchanged numbers, both of us certain we would keep in touch.

In the commotion of deplaning, I was disappointed that I didn't get a chance to properly say goodbye. With our flight arriving a few minutes late, the crew, including myself, rushed off the plane and headed to our next while Max headed to his.

Less than ten minutes later as I arrived at the gate with the same crew sans Max, my phone dinged with a text.

Sorry, I had to rush to catch my next flight. It was amazing meeting you and I can't wait to see you again!

I'm not quite sure why, but following his text, Max sent a headshot of himself without a mustache. His clean-shaven face brightened his eyes and revealed a boyish, almost sexy grin. He looked good and much younger.

Gay or straight, Max was a cool guy that I looked forward to flying with again.

Over the next few weeks, we sent friendly texts back and forth to each other. His tone kept getting friendlier, and even flirty with compliments about my appearance as he remembered it. Eventually, I sent him a few pictures of myself, of my travels, along with a link to my blog. Which, to my surprise, he read and said he enjoyed. It took me a few days to realize that, yup, this man was definitely flirting with me.

"I'd like to take you to dinner the next time you're out this way," he declared during one of our phone conversations. Max would often call me in between his flights and whenever he found himself briefly flying through Chicago.

A few days later, before departure, I texted Max to let him know I got a trip and would be sitting around Los Angeles for a few hours. Having just gotten back from a reserve trip and into his only off day, Max and I coordinated him picking me up from LAX as soon as I arrived so we could go to dinner nearby.

With only an hour-and-a-half for dinner, I met him downstairs in baggage claim pick-up area. It had been less than two weeks since we had first met, yet he jumped out of his green Prius to hug me as if we had not seen each other in years. Not quite as excited as he was, I couldn't help but return the warm embrace.

Over dinner, we continued our various conversations from the plane. I learned that along with being married and divorced, he had a teenage daughter, who was eventually coming to visit him from Australia. He was new to the company as well as to Los Angeles. He enjoyed the climate that allowed him to swim and surf when not on call. For extra money and to break up the boredom, he also drove for Uber. Although far from wealthy, Max shared with me that he owned several properties back home, including a beach house in Japan. But, the pay as a flight attendant to cover his day-to-day expenses was still ridiculously low in comparison to his previous occupations. His experiences as a foreigner, getting familiar with Americans as both a driver and flight attendant, were hilarious. Like me several years earlier, creating a new life in a totally new world was exciting, sometimes confusing. And as a reserve, creating a new life was also frequently exhausting and more frustrating than expected.

A week later, on a Saturday, Max was back through Chicago and on his way to Cleveland for a sixteen-hour layover. He invited me to come along. My Saturday-night date had just flaked, so I was suddenly available. I packed a backpack and met him at the gate of his flight. It was day two of a three-day trip for Max and his crew. Naturally, the LA-based crew, none of whom I had met before, had become great friends by the time I joined them for the Chicago-to-Cleveland leg. Apparently, Max had spoken about me because not only were they aware I would be joining them for the thirty-minute flight but they were also especially friendly, as if they knew how much Max and I liked each other. Throughout the flight, when I wasn't standing in the galley keeping Max company while he worked, the crew, consisting of two older women and one young man, were giving me knowing smiles when they past by my seat as if I was his girlfriend.

When we landed in Cleveland at eleven that night, Max and I, having already eaten on the plane, were ready to relax together in the hotel room. I wasn't nervous or had any expectations of what it would mean for he and I to spend the night together. We talked as he got out of his uniform jacket and shirt and laid down next to me. After a long day of working, he was surprisingly not as tired as I would have been.

I can't recall who kissed who, but our first kiss was filled with an affection and lightheartedness that turned into a playful passion. We'd been in the hotel room for less than an hour before we started making out and taking off our clothes. Hours later, after having sex multiple times, I was absolutely certain that Max was definitely, absolutely, positively, no way in hell, gay. His sensitive and unabashed affection, attentiveness, and casualness in sex was definitely a European thing.

Max and I happily awoke the next morning, lying naked in each other's arms, talking as if we had been a longtime couple. We had known each other for only a few weeks and seen each other a handful of times, but there was a sense of fun and normalcy in our inaugural sex life.

"I don't expect you to say this back right now, but I love who you are," he said as he kissed me. He said it in such a matter of fact and easy way that surprised me. He was different than so many of the men I dated, who had trouble articulating their feelings.

I was flattered. There were a lot of things I really liked about him, but love seemed a bit premature. Although we knew a lot about one another, we had only been "dating" for a short time. Yet, Max did not seem to be playing any games with me and we already knew that he didn't have to say anything to persuade me to sleep with him. He did not need me to even respond about how I felt in that moment, which I appreciated. I chalked it up to Max being older with an openness I truly admired. His unreserved nature and intuitiveness seemed to serve him well.

Despite my reservations about my feelings for Max, I knew I could see myself with this man for a while. I liked the fact that I was not infatuated or enamored with him in a romantic, corny kind of way. I simply wanted to get to know more and more about him. If he really liked me, I thought to myself, he'd wait for my feelings to catch up with his.

I gave him a sincere smile of appreciation before kissing him on the lips.

"Thank you," I said before laying my head back down on his chest, which made him smile. We had fifteen minutes before I had to leave and catch my flight back to Chicago and he had a couple of hours before his return to Los Angeles.

For the next six weeks, Max and I surprisingly saw each other with regularity considering the distance. After I finished my last two work trips for the month, I flew back out to Los Angeles to stay with him for his few off days. During our time together in LA, Max toured me around to areas I hadn't seen, we went hiking, and he gave me a swimming lesson at the community pool in his neighborhood. Although I wasn't vegan, I enjoyed the meals he prepared and the restaurants where we ate. At the end of my visit, we made plans for him to meet me at my place in Mexico during his next few days off. We started talking about travel plans to Israel, Australia, and Japan in the coming summer months. When we were away from each other, we FaceTimed daily.

BLOG POST: RECIPE FOR LOVE

Chi Mc Fly | June 12, 2018 | Released to Crew Rest

Although it takes quite a bit of work to gather all the ingredients, once you have them, this is a fun, easy-to-make recipe, and quite healthy. I hear it goes great with a variety of side dishes including travel, adventure, and much more.

For this flavorful recipe you will need:

- 2 flight attendants (in this recipe, it's one male and one female)
- 1,746 miles between their respective bases in Los Angeles and Chicago
- Short layovers and a few hours of sit time for dating (sit time: 1 to 4 hours you're sitting in the airport between flights)

- 1 or more jump seats on oversold flights to and from Mexico during Spring Break
- 2 cups of kissy-face emojis
- 3 cups of smiley-face emojis
- Solid Wi-Fi signal
- FaceTime
- 4 or more off days for both flight attendants
- 1 large iguana

Directions:

1. In a large metal tube that flies through the air, preheat relationship to 125 degrees (or 2 hours of flight time) using good conversation on a jump seat between two flight attendants who have never met before.

2. Next, combine solid Wi-Fi signal, Facetime conversations, and text messages. In equal amounts, gradually add kissy and smiley-face emojis to text messages. Stir well.

3. Over several weeks, fold in countless days of travel with short layovers, red-eye flights, and sit time in Chicago and Los Angeles to see one another.

4. In a warm climate (Mexico highly recommended) with only walking distance to a beach, allow flight attendants to sit, eat, and sleep side by side for four or more consecutive non-working days. Let marinate.

5. Sprinkle liberal amounts of good conversation, laughter, and real-time kisses.

6. Reduce heat and allow to simmer after wandering through Old Town Puerto Vallarta, hangry and trying to find something for dinner that appeals to both flight attendants. When he wants a veggie buffet in a casual Mexican cafeteria-style dining atmosphere and you're in the mood for an upscale gringo restaurant that serves wine, firmly decide that the upscale

vegetarian gringo restaurant with wine will be where the two of you eat.

7. Kiss and make up after vegan chocolate mousse is served and both are pleased with the meal. Repeat once he says that you have an irrational fear of the almost-invisible iguana that's scurrying around in the thatched roof of the casita. Give him the side-eye when he tries to tell you that it will not jump down from its hiding place and onto your face in the middle of the night.

8. When his visit comes to an end, make plans to go to Los Angeles next week to see one another.

Serves: 2

Calories: not sure, but it's pretty healthy

DEPARTURES

It was the last night of a three-day trip visiting Max in Los Angeles. The time we spent together had been peaceful and fun as usual, but once again, not enough. We had been seeing each other for less than three months, but it felt like a lot longer.

During my off days, I was still going back and forth from Chicago to Mexico, but I added stints to Los Angeles when I could. So far, we had been successful with coordinating our off days even though summer travel was picking up.

Other than recurring tension about when and where to eat since he was vegan and I was not, we enjoyed each other's company. Our time together, hiking and touring the city was filled with affection, smiles, and engaging conversations.

On our final night, as we lay in bed while he awaited his work assignment for the next day, Max asked me about he and I officially being a couple.

"I thought we already were," I said, with my head on his chest as he absentmindedly stroked my arm. Since I met Max,

I hadn't bothered going on occasional random dates. Perhaps he thought I had more suitors than I did, but even when I thought about seeing someone, the only person that ever came to mind was him.

"True," he said. "But, I want to see you as much as I can and my schedule makes it challenging for us. I don't like leaving you,"

"I know, dear. Me neither. We can figure it out. From experience, being on reserve is hard. I wouldn't mind transferring eventually out here."

"Really?"

I nodded. "I've always enjoyed it out here – it was my second choice. But, I can't promise you I'll ever be totally vegan, but I want to eat healthier anyway."

"I will never dictate what you wear or what you eat."

"Then I think we can do this."

"Me too. Let's do it."

We rolled onto our side to spoon with my back pressed against his chest, in what had become our customary sleeping position. His arms tangled up over mine. I turned around to look at his face. A few months ago, he shaved off his mustache again, and since I liked it, he decided to remain hairless.

"If you can go without a mustache though, I can go without meat," I said, making him laugh. "By the way, I love you too, but you know that right?"

"Yes, Love. I do," he said, yawning.

Within a few minutes, he and I were both asleep.

It had been a while since I felt this happy and secure.

Waking up late, we both rushed to get dressed and leave his apartment to get to the airport in time for his morning assignment. At midnight, he had been assigned a trip to D.C. He would be gone for two days and I needed to get back to Chicago. I softly stroked his hand as we rode in silence on the 5 a.m. shuttle that was taking us from the LAX employee parking lot to the terminal. I had slept well but could tell he hadn't because he was quiet.

"You okay?" I asked.

"I can't do this," he replied softly.

I squeezed his hand. Although not a quick call, five hours' notice for a five-hour trip was tough and I knew from experience. I felt bad for Max. He and I were both tired, but at least I could sleep on my flight back to Chicago.

"This isn't going to work," he said looking off into the distance, thinking, and then into my eyes.

I somehow knew he wasn't talking about the job. He was talking about us.

Before I could ask any questions, the van pulled up to the terminal and we grabbed our luggage.

"Okay, what won't work?" I said.

"The distance, the job, you and I. This is all too much. I'm so sorry."

I was thoroughly confused, but getting scared.

What the fuck? What is he talking about?

Max had fifteen minutes to get to his gate to check-in. A crowded airport was not a place to have this discussion.

We walked in silence through the airport to the employee security line. I wracked my brain, searching for a different version of last night. I showed my badge to the officer and proceeded to the right. Max showed his badge and was selected for random additional screening. The officer directed him to the left.

I waited at the top of the escalator with my luggage, leaning against a pillar overlooking the security lines. I watched as he heaved his luggage onto the conveyor belt and pushed it through the x-ray machine. The TSA officer opened his backpack and ever so slowly pulled out the contents of his luggage. Max's forehead wrinkled and a pensive frown that I'd rarely seen covered his face.

My early morning grogginess had now dissipated and was being replaced by a thick, slowly growing lump in my throat. I knew that if we talked about whatever was wrong, it could be resolved. I watched as he ascended the escalator. His normally shining eyes that were purposely avoiding mine were dimmed. I stood defeated in disbelief as he kissed me goodbye on the lips, slowly, softly, apologetically.

"I'm running late. I have to go," he somberly said. I said nothing. I was still too stunned. I didn't know what to say or what could be said. I had to go. I knew he had to go. He hugged me. I didn't hug back.

We were walking in the same direction, but I understood it was his way of saying he didn't want to walk together any further. My pace and the growing state of sadness were slowing both of us down to get to our flights.

My brain came back online as he walked away.

We would sort this out later, I thought. Besides, in that moment, without talking to him, it didn't make any sense based on what happened in the night for him to change his mind.

It didn't cross my mind either that I wouldn't see Max again. I couldn't fathom he wouldn't kiss me again. We wouldn't travel to Japan or Prague together as we planned. I wouldn't meet his family. He wouldn't meet mine.

But, after going our separate ways at the LAX airport that day, Max and I never saw each other in person again. When we spoke later that evening, he was tired and not feeling well. The next day, he had a fever and just wanted to sleep. Understanding the exhaustion of reserve life, I tabled our needed conversation and just Facetimed the following few days to simply check on him. He looked horrible; his beautiful face was clammy and pale. When I offered to come back out to Los Angeles to take care of him, he declined.

A week later when Max was feeling better, we started speaking again. But something felt different. Our conversations were fragile and Max was determined to stick to his unilateral decision.

"It has nothing to do with you," he said. "I need to figure out what I'm doing with my life. A relationship with you is not the answer I thought it was."

I was still confused. Nothing he said made sense.

For the next two weeks, we had a series of sporadic and awkward Facetime chats and texts. Many of our calls were filled with me crying and him apologizing before hurriedly getting off the phone. It felt as if he had tricked me, made me trust him, even fall in love with him, and then he simply changed his mind. I told him so and he repeatedly said that that wasn't the case, but never offered an explanation. As I got angry for answers he thought he had given, our conversations ended.

For about a month, I thought Max would come to his senses. We would work out whatever was going on. Something would change. The theories from my friends ranged from he was scared to commit to he wasn't really divorced. Neither of those seemed likely, unless my judge of character was so poor to the point it might as well have been nonexistent. Had I been living in a self-created illusion that Max genuinely cared about me? Or, was it that I let him see too much of who I really was and was too scared to admit that he didn't like what he saw? I was probably the stupid one to have fallen for him. I shouldn't have let my guard down.

Eventually, Max and I stopped talking altogether. I couldn't make him explain to me in a way I could understand or accept. All that was left were more questions.

Had our entire relationship been simply a fling?

Was he simply a flake?

What had I done?

What had I not done?

What was wrong with me?

I questioned if he had ever really loved me. Had I even loved him or was I simply infatuated? What else was I to expect from an Australian-German-engineer turned shamanic-trainee turned flight-attendant? I settled on the fact that he was a flaky, abstract, hippy womanizer who flowed wherever the wind blew.

This seemed like an inadequate reason as all the others.

As hard as it was to accept, I simply settled on the fact that Max, as unexpectedly as he came into my life, unexpectedly and suddenly departed.

LIFE AS A CORPORATE MUGGLE

"Girl, you're on the go too much. Men don't want that. They want someone who's stable," said my married college friend. A newlywed and now a relationship coach, Kendra was giving me advice on how to get a man.

I never took her advice too seriously; a conventional man is something I never wanted. Otherwise, I would have married Eric, the sweet guy with little ambition who I dated for two years after college. We met at an electronics store in the mall where he worked as the assistant manager. More than anything, Eric wanted a family of his own, a mini-van, and a home with a white picket fence. He sheepishly admitted to me one day that if I wanted to stay barefoot and pregnant, that would be perfectly okay with him.

I saw it coming but was still hurt when we broke up several months later. He cheated on me with his coworker and got her pregnant. She was more the barefoot-and-pregnant type I guess.

Approaching forty, I was still single and once again recovering from heartbreak.

Maybe I did need to settle down in one place for a while, but not for the sake of attracting a man. Max, during one of our several confusing post-breakup conversations, mentioned the thought of me always traveling without him made him sad. He was a flight attendant as well, so once again, I didn't quite understand. But, being honest with myself, as much as I initially enjoyed living in the two worlds of Chicago and Puerto Vallarta, it was beginning to wear on me. I could feel the stress creeping in no matter where I geographically was at any given moment.

On top of that, it was early May again, and the Chicago summer would soon be in full swing. Rather than head right away to Mexico after my work trips, I found myself lingering in Chicago, wanting to attend an outdoor festival or get some time in on the lakefront with friends. I didn't look forward to returning for my second rainy season in Mexico. It was too hot and humid to do much other than sit under a fan all day. To make matters worse, during especially heavy rains (which was usually every other day), the palapa roof of the casita leaked. Unlike my sudden breakup with Max, I knew my time in Mexico was coming to an end.

On the job front, further complicating matters were rumors the company was cutting back on staffing. There was a possibility that I could be on reserve again, which would mean I wouldn't have enough time or energy to go back and forth to Mexico either. Just the thought of being on reserve caused me anxiety. While I was certain I still enjoyed my job and all that it allowed, I felt as if I needed a break from the flight-attendant lifestyle for a while.

As I was contemplating all this, and what to do next, an internal job posting for a year-long position at the company's downtown Chicago office arrived in my company email inbox.

They were specifically looking for flight attendants within the company to participate in special administrative projects. Upon completion of the projects, flight attendants could go back to flying. The job requirements for the special assignment matched my pre-flight attendant skills to a tee, which prompted me to apply. Without having to permanently give up flying, I could give this stability thing a go.

Besides, there could be perks to an office job. As a starter, the job paid considerably more without having to travel as much. Then, I'd be able to comfortably afford my own apartment, should I need to be in Chicago every day. In Mexico, I had started to enjoy my alone time without roommates. Although Violet was still gone quite a bit, she eventually found a second renter for the larger room. Cary, the new roommate, was always home. She was friendly enough, but I didn't care for her much. She seemed a bit off for a reason I couldn't figure out. Maybe it had something to do with the fact that she was six feet tall with a baby voice that sounded fake and slightly creepy.

At an office, there would probably be more order and predictability, like weekly staff meetings and set lunch breaks. I could be okay working with the same people day in and out. Maybe it would be like that TV show, *The Office,* or that Dilbert comic strip. The dark irony would keep me laughing. I could decorate my cubicle with plants and pictures of my family. Or maybe, I would just get a bunch of cat posters to annoy people.

I would be home every night or almost every night. Instead of packing and unpacking luggage in the evenings, I'd go to happy hours where maybe I'd even meet more professionals and we'd have things in common. I'd get a chance to wear the business professional clothes that I hadn't worn in years (that is, if they still fit). I would be able to have a regular gym routine, something else I hadn't had in years. I could train my body to get up super-early in the morning to work out before showering and dressing for work. I would effortlessly lose twenty pounds by eating lunch at the same time every day with the same group of people.

On Saturday nights, perhaps I'd hang out at the Chicago clubs when I didn't have a hot date that I could always schedule and confirm. I'd always do my laundry and grocery shopping on Sunday rather than a random weekday in the middle of the morning with the senior citizens. I heard that at grocery stores on Sundays, there were more cute guys roaming the aisles anyway. On holiday weekends, instead of working or fighting to get the day off, I could leave work early like everyone else and go on a road trip.

Yes, I'd be giving up a considerable amount of flexibility, freedom, and work autonomy. If I didn't like it, I knew that eventually it would end. In the meantime, I'd make the best of it.

I easily got the job, as I expected. My roommates, eager for me to move out or pay more rent, wanted to know all the details even before I got the job. The details I didn't know, but I promised I would fill them as soon as I knew. For the past month, I had been in town more often than they wanted and paying an unequal fraction of the rent. We'd been getting into text "discussions" on who left the bathroom a mess and how to properly load the dishwasher. The frequency of nice-nasty Post-it notes was increasing. My vegan roommates were repulsed by the chicken that I kept in the fridge. I was repulsed by their smoking habits. As soon as I found out that I landed the job, I sent them a text informing them that I would be moving out by the end of the month.

Using an apartment finder service instead of Craigslist this time, I found a studio apartment in a Chicago neighborhood called Lakeview. It was an upscale, but still affordable area with tons of gourmet restaurants, cafes, theaters, and boutique shops. Everything was within walking distance – the "L," the cleaners, the grocery store, and the pharmacy. A lot of flight attendants lived in the area due to the ease of getting to the airport in less than an hour and downtown within thirty minutes. Best of all, it was within walking distance to the lakefront. Although I had abandoned my Mexican beach, I still had water nearby.

By now, I had grown accustomed to perpetual states of change and transition. I had a new vision and would try to make it as exciting as Mexico. Life as a corporate muggle could work. While waking up during the first few weeks and getting out of the apartment on time proved more difficult than I thought it would be, I enjoyed the morning commute that consisted of walking a block to catch a crowded train. The energy of the downtown morning rush hour with people everywhere hustling and bustling beneath ginormous skyscrapers energized me.

Once in the office, I got into a rhythm, walking past the same people in the same cubicles and saying good morning. The work I was assigned engaged my brain and challenged me. I had a chance to understand business operations and gained a greater appreciation for my duties on the plane. I enjoyed working alongside my supervisor, who was an accomplished businesswoman. She was fair-minded and strategic and knew how to work with all different types of people. I enjoyed our meetings and the people on the project team. But, knowing I was only a visitor in the corporate world, I kept my overachieving nature at bay. When I was in the office, I worked hard, but didn't feel the need to always stay late. On most days, I left promptly at 5:30 p.m. I had things to do, which included working on my writing business.

A couple of months into the year-long assignment, the pace and intensity of the work picked up. I still enjoyed the work and was fully engaged, but by the evenings, I was drained. I didn't want to do anything but go home, eat dinner, and watch TV until I fell asleep. Most of the time, I didn't feel like exercising out or spending more time at a computer finding new writing clients. Although I wasn't physically tired as I was after a trip, I was mentally drained after eight and nine hours under fluorescent office lights.

Surprisingly, time was tight, scrambling on weekends to run all my errands, which included grocery shopping and cooking a few meals for the week. I had yet to get into a routine. Some weeks, I brought my food to work, although lunch time was never the same. I worked out in the office's executive gym on the mornings when I woke up in time to pack a change of clothes and toiletries, which varied from week to week. Corporate life out of the office wasn't coming together as smoothly or as quickly as I envisioned. My social life outside of work had yet to improve. I was in a new neighborhood and figured it would take some time. Although I occasionally attended after-work functions with coworkers as well as a few Black professional networking events on my own, I often found them boring and left early.

Weekends always snuck up on me and I rarely had anything planned. I still didn't feel like getting on a plane and traveling either. I didn't want to be bothered with having to compete with other weekend travel warriors and have the stress of not getting back for work on time. So, I stayed put and puttered around the neighborhood or just relaxed by the lake reading. Every now and then, I hung out with my few Chicago friends, my cousins, or Marsha and Miguel. But more often, I found myself without much to do on the weekends. By the time the weekend loneliness settled in, it was time to go back to work.

Despite my efforts, my dating life sucked. I was tired of the short-term, sporadic activity buddies that I met online. Usually, they were bored after a recent breakup and just looking for temporary companionship or a friends-with-benefits situation. They'd usually reveal this information after the first or second date, which was usually a ho-hum meetup for drinks or coffee.

While I had a few lunch dates with men who worked downtown, I quickly realized they were inconvenient due to the unpredictability of my lunch hour. Sometimes, although I would plan for noon to meet a new guy for lunch a few blocks from the office, my day-to-day schedule would quickly change. I'd have to either reschedule or reluctantly tear myself away from my desk. When I did the latter, I was usually running to get to and from lunch. I was not focused, or in the mood to put my best foot forward with someone I barely knew. After a couple of lunch dates with boring, yet professional men, I decided to take a break from online dating altogether. At the same time, I wasn't going out much to social events to meet anyone. All the men in the office were either married, gay, or just plain unattractive.

Work, Netflix, and sleep kept me occupied on most weekdays and weekends during the first couple of months. So, not having much of a social life really didn't matter. I was still optimistic that eventually, I would find my corporate muggle rhythm. I just needed to give it more time. I was still content with my decision to take a break from flying.

DIVERSIONS

"Craig, something isn't right with her."

"What do you mean?"

"She was sleeping a lot and breathing funny."

"Well, she's getting older. Older people sleep more"

I sighed and rolled my eyes.

"No, Craig. I was just there. She didn't look right. She was sleeping after she had just woke up and having trouble breathing when she was sitting down. Have you even talked to your mother lately?"

It was early Sunday evening and I was on the phone, talking to my brother. I had just returned from visiting with my mother in Atlanta. It had been several months since I last visited due to starting my new in-office job. Despite not wanting to spend the too-short weekends non-revving to Atlanta, I knew I needed to go see for myself how she was doing. For the past two months, my mother had been sick at an unusual frequency. Her breathing, when I spoke to her over the phone, always sounded labored as if she'd been racing up a flight of stairs to answer it.

"No, it's not a big deal," she said without opening her eyes. "I'm just tired, I didn't sleep well."

After my mother's bypass surgery during my senior college year, Craig and I were used to her moving a bit slower, and regularly going to the doctor for monitoring. About once or twice a year, the doctor would admit her to the hospital due to blood pressure issues. They'd run tests to make sure that she didn't have any blockage in her heart, and if she did, they'd perform a routine procedure to clear the artery. However, over the past two months, she'd been in and out of the hospital and doctors' offices every few weeks.

At first, I figured her exhaustion was probably just due to all the traveling she and my stepfather Curtis did over the summer. The beauty of working for the airlines is that not only can I, as a flight attendant, travel for free, but also my spouse, boyfriend (if I had one), and immediate family members, including my parents, could travel for almost-free too. I loved being able to give my mother and stepfather the gift of travel. It gave them a chance to visit other family members who lived all across the country. With a bit of coaching and me as their travel agent, booking their flights, they navigated flying standby with ease. As I instructed, she and my stepfather arrived early to the airport, requested a wheelchair for my mom, and slowly made their way to the gates. Although getting older and despite her condition, the two of them still traveled a few times a year. My mother, who knew how to manage her health, was in good enough shape to travel most of the time, and knew when she wasn't up for it.

I enjoyed hearing about her travels as much as she enjoyed hearing about mine. During most of my childhood, my mother, although she liked to travel, did so only by car. For as long as I remember, she was scared of flying. Several times she would talk about perhaps taking a plane somewhere, but usually at the last minute we would end up driving.

It was ironic too that my mother had never been on a plane, especially since my grandfather worked at Detroit Metro Airport for decades as a skycap. As I do now, he had buddy passes, which my aunts, uncles, and cousins frequently used. In fact, it was my grandfather, not my mother, who took my brother and I on our first plane ride to California when I was seven years old and my brother was ten.

Before then, we'd become used to traveling around the country with our mother by car. During summer vacations and holidays, we took road trips from Michigan to Alabama, where most of my mother's family lived. During the one, sometimes two-day drive, if we stopped and spent the night along the way, my brother and I sat in the back of the car, bickering, playing the license plate game, or getting passing trucks to blow their horns while my mother took turns driving with one of my uncles. When my uncles weren't available to ride south or back to Michigan, it would be just the three of us. My mother, in her late twenties and into her early thirties, would hit the road with her two young kids, who argued at rest stops about who would ride shotgun. Most of the time, my brother would win since I was more than likely to fall asleep and leave the driver on her own in the front to keep herself awake.

Eventually, when Craig and I were older and away in college, my mother signed up for a class offered by the airlines to help people with a fear of flying. After recovering from her heart attack in her early fifties, she retired from teaching middle school and became a national education consultant, helping other teachers. The job sometimes involved long-distance travel. She recognized that not getting on a plane limited her opportunities.

The class explained aircraft noises and what happens during the different phases of flight such as takeoff and landing. The course also taught breathing and relaxation techniques to help manage anxiety. Graduation included a short thirty-minute flight from Detroit to Chicago that my mother successfully completed. From that point on, although still nervous from time to time, she started traveling by plane, but still preferred to drive rather than fly whenever she could.

Although she and Curtis flew once that summer and did short road trips most of the time, I suspected another reason for my mother's present condition was also due to grief. It had been less than a year since my grandmother passed away and we were all grieving. While we all were figuratively heartbroken over her loss, I grew worried that my mother was physically heartbroken as well. It was scary to think that grief, coupled with a weakened heart condition, could take its toll. It would explain her prolonged state of "not feeling too well" as she called it, which this time included a loss of appetite and the need to sleep sitting upright in order to breathe better. My stepfather, who was often the one taking her back and forth to the doctor since they got married four years ago, was worried as well. It was alarming and frustrating that after a day or two in the hospital, the doctors, after checking for blockages and adjusting her medications, sent her home. A week or two later, when she was still not feeling any better, she'd go back to the hospital while awaiting her appointment to see a specialist the following month.

Had I still been flying instead of working in an office, it would be easier to get the days off to stay longer in Atlanta or visit with more frequency. Without having to report to anyone or get approval first, I could have been at the hospital and gone with her and Curtis to doctor's appointments on short notice. The nine-to-five corporate schedule was similar to reserve flight attendant life in that my time was not always my own. Even if I wasn't working, I had to be in Chicago. It was around November. With the holidays approaching and projects needing to be finished, I worked later in the evenings to get ahead so I could lump my few allotted vacation days together and go home early for Thanksgiving to beat the holiday rush.

Although Craig initially planned to spend Christmas in Detroit with his wife's family, I was thankful that at the last minute that he heeded my suggestion and spent a few days after Christmas in Atlanta. It had been over a decade since both of her children had been home at the same time. Due to it being so last minute, my sister-in-law Dominique and the kids couldn't adjust their travel plans. Plus, kids running around if my mother wasn't feeling too well was probably not the best thing. But, I knew having my brother and me there would lift my mother's grieving spirit and I wanted my brother to tell me if I was being overly concerned.

For a few days, it was just the four of us: Craig, Curtis, my mother, and me. She was excited to have us home and looked much better than she sounded on the phone, but still not quite as energetic as I had seen her on other occasions. Before we arrived, she informed us that she wasn't up for cooking much. This was unusual, but understandable as the first Christmas without our grandmother, who lived with my mother and Curtis before she died. Instead of turkey, we had beef ribs, a few side dishes, and one sweet potato pie. Post-Christmas dinner was nice and uneventful. Without my brother's family, my grandmother, and other family members who my mother usually invited over for holiday dinners, it was the smallest and quietest holiday we'd ever spent together.

My mother's condition continued to get worse over the next month. Finally, in mid-January, she had a second appointment with a heart specialist. They scheduled her for another heart surgery. This time, instead of simply clearing a blockage, which normally improved her condition, they would need to do a much more complicated procedure to completely replace a rapidly deteriorating valve. To my surprise, the surgery was quickly scheduled to take place within a few weeks. Although at the time, I didn't understand completely what the surgery would do, I knew that I needed time off to be there.

My boss understood that I would need to use the remainder of my vacation time and possibly more to be with my mother during the surgery. In exchange for a few extra days off, I'd agreed to remotely work as much as I could to keep my projects moving. We were short-staffed and more deadlines were looming.

No one on the team was thrilled by my absence at such a critical point in the project, but they all understood.

I flew in on the night before her surgery, which would take place on a Tuesday morning. After working all day on Monday, I left work and headed straight to the airport. After landing, I rented a car and drove straight to the hospital. I arrived at around 11 p.m. that night, after visiting hours. My brother and stepfather had gone home for the evening, but the nurses, knowing I had just flown in, let me spend some time with her. My mother was feeling better and relaxed from the medication to prep her for the next day. She said was looking forward to the relief that she hoped the surgery could provide. I stayed and chatted with her before she fell asleep.

Even though I was utterly exhausted from a day of long office work and airplane travel, there was no point in getting a hotel for only a few hours of sleep. I wasn't up for driving to my mother's house on the other side of town either, so I stayed in the hospital waiting room. I would be the first to see her in the morning when she woke up and before they wheeled her into surgery around six a.m. The nurse gave me hospital sheets and blankets that I spread out on a hard series of armless chairs. Too nervous and uncomfortable to sleep, I laid there for a few hours, listening to noisy beeping monitors from the patient rooms and the shuffling rubber soles of nurses walking about.

The next morning, my mother was wheeled off to prep for surgery before Curtis and Craig arrived. Before they put her to sleep, Curtis and Craig got a chance to quickly see her off. During the hours while we waited, Curtis shared more details about her condition during the past several months. Neither my brother nor I were fully aware of its severity when we saw her over the Christmas holiday, but we knew it wasn't good. He told us about the long nights he stayed awake to make sure she kept breathing. He explained the abnormal amount of swelling due to poor circulation that had caused them to return to the hospital with frequency. The regular cardiologist, before referring her out to another specialist, told both of them that there was nothing more he could do. Her heart was failing and only two options remained: a heart transplant or the next best thing, a heart pump. For a heart transplant, the wait could be indefinite, given her age. The surgery for the pump could be done immediately. Without either procedure, and given the condition of her heart, she only had a few months to live.

The surgery took over ten hours. For most of the day, we were the only family in the spacious cardiac unit waiting room where I had slept the night before. I sat working remotely, which kept my mind occupied for the most part. Craig played on his iPad while Curtis sat reading and occasionally roaming the hospital halls to the vending machines, cafeteria, and outside. In between working, I fielded texts and calls from family members, keeping them updated. The three of us always made sure that one of us stayed in the waiting room at all times near the phone in case the nursing staff called with updates. Every few hours, the phone rang. They called to let us know when the surgery began, when they implanted the heart pump, and how much longer it would be before completion.

In the late afternoon, the nurse who was in charge of my mother's care escorted us through a series of corridors into a smaller, more secluded waiting room. The windowless room was little bit bigger than a closet. It was empty, except for five or six chairs lined up again the walls. There were two doors; the one from which we entered, and on the opposite wall, another door that led to the surgical room. The eggshell-colored walls inside the room were bare. One instinctively knew that this tiny room was the area where critical surgery outcomes were discussed. It was eerily quiet. With the door closed, you couldn't hear any of the regular hospital noises like intercom pages or the shushing of sliding entry/exit doors. There was no beeping, buzzing, and churning of hospital medical machinery. This was the room tucked away from the eyes of strangers and staff, where families received information about the condition of their loved ones. The three of us waited in silence for the doctor, each of us in our own worlds of fear.

Thirty minutes after we arrived in the room, a doctor wearing green scrubs walked in from the surgical unit door. He introduced himself as Dr. Markenson to my brother and I. Curtis had met him previously, and I had heard his name mentioned by Curtis and my mother on several occasions. Dr. Markenson was a towering, white older man who instantly commanded the room. He had wire-rimmed glasses, gray hair, and a moderate amount of forehead wrinkles. He looked exactly like I expected a doctor to look. He had a friendly manner that exuded experience and expertise.

Dr. Markenson took a seat in one of the chairs. He sighed and removed his surgical cap as if he was sitting down after a long day of work on his feet. He hunched over and leaned in, preparing for a weighty conversation. Before he began speaking, I searched his face to determine if he was preparing to deliver good or bad news. I couldn't tell. He proceeded to give us a play-by-play of the surgery, which involved placing my mother's heart on bypass and a blood transfusion. Half of his explanation I didn't understand.

"The surgery was a success," he finally said after a few minutes of explaining the details. I let out the breath that I had been holding and blinked back tears of relief. "I expect her to start waking up with the next few hours. We'll monitor her closely in the next forty-eight hours, which will be the ultimate test. But so far, she's stable and doing well. They're bringing her into the ICU right now and you can go in and see her in about fifteen minutes."

As slowly as he sat down, Dr. Markenson rose from the chair. We solemnly shook his hand and thanked him.

As the doctor left, the three of us kept sitting in silence and relief.

Within ten minutes, a nurse came through the door that led to the operating rooms and escorted us through to the post-surgery ICU. My mother had just been wheeled into the area and another nurse hovered around her, casually hooking her up to monitors and IVs. The three of us quietly tiptoed to the end of her bed. The nurse warmly smiled encouraging us to come closer and gather around her. Tubes were taped into her nostrils and her mouth. Except for the breathing machine moving air in and out of her body, she lay motionless. Her face was a color I had never seen before. It was ashen gray and swollen to twice its normal size. It did not look like my mother, but rather, a corpse. I reminded myself that the doctor had just said that she did well, although it sure didn't look like it. The three of us were scared to breathe for fear of disturbing her fragile body. Instead, we intently stared at her and listened to the machines that were beeping, indicating signs of life.

"Delores," the nurse said firmly and happily as if attempting to command her awake. "Your family is here," she said, gently rubbing her shoulder. My mother didn't respond. The nurse didn't seem concerned nor worried.

"It's going to take her a while for the anesthesia to wear off," said the nurse.

She could tell the three of us were still trying to take in my mother's appearance. Her demeanor and response to our reaction indicated that she had frequently dealt with post-surgery patients and their families.

"Delores," she loudly repeated as if my mother was deaf instead of unconscious. "Can you wiggle your toes for me?"

Our eyes darted directly to the feet that stuck out from under the thin sheet draped on her body. There wasn't any movement. The three of us stopped breathing once again. The nurse repeated her order, slightly louder. Our eyes stayed glued to her small, size eight feet. There was the faintest of movement of her big toe. Then it moved again. The nurse was pleased. "There you go!"

"Hi, Ma," I said. The toe moved again. After that the three of us gently brushed my mother's toes to say goodbye before we left to let her rest. The nurse informed us that it would be a long while before the anesthesia wore off enough for her to open her eyes. We left the ICU, silent, but walking a bit lighter. We headed to the house to get some rest after a draining day.

After a shower and a few hours of sleep, I left the house early the next morning and headed to the hospital before Craig and Curtis got up. I wanted to be there when she woke up. By the time I arrived, they had just moved her out of the ICU and into a regular recovery room. Two nurses were moving about, unhooking the breathing machine to get her repaired heart working again on its own. Thinking it seemed a bit soon to be moving her about, I watched as the nurses quickly heaved her body upright with startling precision. My mother's still swollen eyes popped open in surprise at the movement before drooping back down. Sitting upright as they checked her vitals, she fell back to sleep. Over the next few days, she continued to sleep, waking up for a few minutes at a time to briefly talk before falling back to sleep. She'd sit with her eyes closed and talk for a few minutes before nodding off.

For the week while she recovered, I continued working remotely from the chair in the corner of her room. Although I expected to be gone for only a couple of days, I informed my job that it would be a few more days before I could return. My mother was still groggy and I was not yet convinced that she was out of the woods. The swelling in her face started to gradually decrease. As family and friends came to visit her, she was awake and alert for longer and longer periods. I helped feed her, watched the nurses change her bandages, and shooed family out of the room when she needed rest. It would still be a few weeks before she would be able to go home, but slowly and surely, she was coming back to life.

On the day I planned to leave, I decided to catch the 10 a.m. flight. As the day went on, I wasn't ready to leave my mother's side. I pushed my flight back to 2 p.m. and extended the car rental. By 4 p.m., I started to tell her that I would be leaving soon, although I then stayed for another two hours. I was cutting it close to catch the last flight out for the day, but I wanted to see her wake up a bit more.

"Staying longer isn't going to make it any easier to leave," she murmured as she went back into a deep sleep.

I knew she was right. I had to get back to work. But I knew, as the daughter, I was supposed to take care of my mother. I felt so guilty for leaving once again. Eventually, I kissed my sleeping mother goodbye and told her I'd return over the weekend before slowly gathering my things and leaving.

For the entire week, I called Curtis every day, sometimes a couple times a day, to see how she was doing. Sometimes, he was at the hospital when I called. Sometimes, he was at the house getting rest. The following weekend when I returned, she was more alert, and the doctors were impressed by the speed of her recovery. With a couple months to go on my temporary assignment and my mother still doing well, I went back and forth to Atlanta on weekends with less frequency. I knew Curtis was taking good care of her, which allowed me to finish my last month out strong.

I enjoyed the time in the office and everyone was pleased with my work. They were impressed that I didn't miss a beat with my projects and many constantly inquired about my mother, which was thoughtful. Eventually, as the projects wrapped up, the amount of work slowed to a crawl. I found myself bored, sitting around without much to do. I was ready to get back to flying. During the last month, my boss suggested that I apply for a permanent in-office position, so I did. The job sounded appealing and the pay was lucrative, but I wasn't sure if I wanted to stay working in an office. When the special assignment ended, they were still interviewing other candidates, and a decision on the permanent position I had applied for had not yet been made.

A week after returning to flying, I got a call with a job offer. Pleased with my performance, my boss gave me a glowing recommendation, which helped seal the deal. My new boss, should I accept the position, saw my potential to excel. I thought about the structure and stability the position could provide. The opportunity for professional growth and the higher pay could get me out of debt faster.

After reviewing the pros and cons, I politely declined the offer.

I wanted to go back to flying.

ACT III

DEPRESSION SUCKS

Fall was turning into winter when I returned to work as a flight attendant after not flying for almost a year. I didn't expect to be, but I was nervous on my first trip back. Although I had been with the airlines for almost seven years, it felt like I was a new hire all over again. Packing and getting ready the night before, I checked and double-checked the details of my trip, caught up on new in-flight announcements, and reviewed updated aircraft policies – all things that I hadn't needed to do in a long while. I wasn't sure if I would remember the order of service or the location of the equipment on each aircraft since it had been so long.

Although I was nervous, just like the night before I got my very first assignment, there were a lot of differences with my return to flying. Instead of being in a hotel before my first day, I was in my own apartment. Even though I was back to an hourly wage instead of a salary, my hourly wage finally jumped to a point where, I could comfortably make ends meet with a bit of smart budgeting. The luxury of not having roommates was worth every penny I didn't spend, and any extra hours I needed to fly.

When I reported to the gate mid-morning the next day and stepped onto the aircraft, I realized that working a flight as a flight attendant is like riding a bike; even if you haven't done it in a while, it all comes back quickly. The safety checks, boarding announcements, food prep, and other customer service activities like picking up trash and getting annoyed at customers taking up space in a tiny galley were instinctive. On my first layover in a year, I realized how much I had missed the feeling of walking into a spacious, quiet hotel room after a long duty day and falling into a mountain of fresh pillows on a neatly made bed. I had even missed the camaraderie of grabbing dinner with the crew during layovers.

Although the actual work on the plane hadn't changed, scheduling procedures and the availability of trips was different. Fortunately, the company had not cut back on staffing, but rather expanded. I was still a line holder who could pick and choose which trips I wanted to fly. While getting the time off that I wanted got even easier, finding trips I actually wanted to fly, got a bit harder. At the beginning of every month, I was able to clear my schedule so that I could find trips to fit my preferences. I didn't want to wake up early. I didn't want to sit around airports all-day or work an arduous fifteen-hour-day with multiple legs. I preferred international trips with one long flight over, a one-day layover to recover, and then one leg back to Chicago. And I wanted weekends off.

Those were the kind of trips, however, that most flight attendants wanted, and to get them, you had to move fast. I began to spend my entire day in my apartment, looking for trips on the computer and my phone, often finding them just a few hours before departure. It was almost like being reserve again. This time, I wasn't waiting for a phone to ring; I was packed and waiting on a notification ping, alerting me that a trip I wanted was available in the computer's queue. There were specific times of the day and late at night when available trips popped up in the queue. I had to be watching and ready to snag it before someone else did. If I was too slow the night before or missed the window, I'd have to keep waiting for something to randomly show up during the day. As it got later in the day and I hadn't found a trip, the more anxious I got. If I hadn't snagged anything by 4 p.m. or 5 p.m., when most of the international flights departed, I'd give up and try again the next day.

Along with anxiety, a familiar feeling of loneliness returned. I was frequently home in my small studio apartment during the weekday with nothing to do except constantly check for availability of trips. I started sleeping in later, and when awake, I stayed in bed longer, checking for trips on my phone while watching Netflix on my laptop. Unless I found a trip, I figured there wasn't a reason to get showered or dressed. Unless I was hungry, then I'd then drag myself out of bed and walk to the corner store for junk food. Other times, I just wouldn't eat.

On days when afternoons turned into evenings and I still hadn't found a trip, I'd start thinking about all the stuff I should have done. I should have worked out. I should have cleaned up or ran errands. I should have planned better. But, I just didn't feel like doing anything. Tomorrow, I told myself, I would worry about the money I didn't make. Having been in this space before, I was familiar enough with the signs of depression to recognize when I was slowly or quickly going down such path. I was going slowly, but steadily.

My depressive funk would last for a few days or until I found a trip. It was like I would get a high from getting a trip. I felt useful and productive. My mind was occupied for several days, interacting with crew and customers. On layovers, I focused either on getting sufficient rest, working out in the gym or checking out the city. But when I returned and recovered from a trip, the cycle of sitting around and looking for the next trip began again. Getting a trip became a temporary jolt out of a cycle of depression. Although there were days when I feel better, it never lasted long. Each cycle got worse.

On long stints of off days, when I chose not to distract myself with work, I would catch up with friends or go on online dates. Often, I'd laugh, smile, and have a genuinely good time. It was better than shopping on Amazon and spending money on things I really didn't need, which I sometimes did in hopes that it would make me feel better. Everything was a temporary fix to ignore a nagging sense of uneasiness. I always felt like I should be doing more with my life than just traveling from place to place. There were only so many beach vacations a person could take. On the other hand, I felt that I should be grateful. Others were envious of the life I led. I had the most important thing that so many people lacked: time.

Yet, although I had fun moments of travel and outings with friends, I wasn't feeling happy or fulfilled.

It took several months and a series of actions to get back on track. Having traveled the spiraling path of depression before, my first order of business was to find a therapist I actually liked to help me figure out what was really wrong. With regular sessions with a therapist who held me accountable for going to the gym, I had a starting point for exploring what would bring me lasting joy and fulfillment. My plans to be a millionaire in my thirties had fallen apart, but on the eve of entering my forties, all I wanted was peace of mind.

ALL THE SINGLE LADIES
OVER FORTY

"It was almost perfect," I told my mother over the phone about my birthday party.

I knew if she could, she would've been in attendance to celebrate her "baby" turning forty. Although she still was not completely recovered from her surgery from six months ago, she was getting there. The doctors, still pleased with her progress for her age, told her it would take a least a year to recover from such a major surgery. But, with the replacement valve that got her heart pumping steadily again, she was feeling significantly better and she sounded more and more like herself each day.

Until the night of the party, I'd been feeling some kinda way about this milestone birthday. I wasn't consciously dwelling on the fact that, at forty, I was unmarried and without children. It was such a society-driven cliché, attempting to tell me that there was something terribly wrong with me, and my life. I didn't completely buy into such a notion.

Nevertheless, there was still an undercurrent of sadness that I didn't even have a significant other to host a party on my behalf. Like I did ten years ago when I turned thirty, I'd be once again throwing a party for myself. I dreaded reliving the experience of having to smile and suppress the loneliness that would float to the top when the party ended. This time, I didn't want to be surrounded by distant friends and acquaintances for the sake of a crowd. Nor did I want to go through the stress of planning an event. My birthday celebration would be a simple, intimate gathering with a handful of Chicago family and friends.

One evening while visiting Marsha and Miguel, I was telling them about my uncertainty about the party. I also wanted their feedback on an intimate venue such as a restaurant.

"If the weather is still nice, I'm thinking maybe just having a bonfire at Promontory Park. Would you all come?"

"How about having it here at the house? You can have a fire pit on the patio," said Marsha.

"Really?" The thought of having in the place that I considered my second home hadn't crossed my mind. Had it, I would have never dared to ask, for concern it would be such an intrusive request.

"Yes," said Miguel. "It's been a while since we had a wild party."

"Well, it definitely won't be wild. Probably not a lot of people. I'm thinking about ten. Are you all sure?"

"It will be fun," said Marsha.

I was more excited about a house party now, especially since Marsha and Miguel would get a chance to meet my brother and his family that I talked about often.

On the evening of the party, I arrived at Marsha and Miguel's with party supplies and food, after running around town getting my hair and nails done. The place was beautiful as always. I was delightfully surprised to discover Marsha and

Miguel also prepared food for the party. Nearly all the people I invited and hoped would attend came to celebrate. My brother and sister-in-law trekked from the suburbs to the city with the twins, who kept everyone entertained with their precocious personalities. The crisp fall evening made it perfect as we sat around a fire pit on the patio, roasting marshmallows, drinking wine, and laughing. I was so excited that everyone was having a good time. Marsha was having a good time getting to know all my friends and Miguel was pleased that everyone was drinking his custom-made cocktails.

For the first time since living in Chicago, I had a chance to gather all my friends together in one place. It was exactly the intimate and warm party that I had envisioned for my birthday. The party ended at around two in the morning. Everyone helped clean up. Exhausted, I stayed over at Marsha and Miguel's, and woke up happy about the love of true friends and family that lingered. My fortieth year on the planet was off to a surprisingly good start.

As the year progressed, I continued to watch friends get engaged. I watched other single friends have babies without the involvement of a partner. I was an unofficial auntie to a few of them and watched up close the challenges of being single, forty, and with a kid. I confirmed that, although I wanted a family, a child without a committed partner was not the route I wanted to go. My lifestyle of travel was not a barrier to having kids, but a complex challenge I wouldn't want to figure out alone.

But, part of me was envious of friends whose perspectives on life had shifted. The petty longings were no longer of importance. Their life's purpose had come into such sharp focus. I wanted that. Although their day-to-day lives were difficult, they were driven by something bigger than themselves.

Meanwhile, I was sitting on beaches, talking with a therapist and taking hikes, trying to figure it all out. The unanswered questions that had been gnawing at my spirit since I returned to flying still lingered. Yet, the process of finding the answers was no longer this overwhelming, impossible task. It simply required me to explore more possibilities – something I was getting really good at. Eventually, I'd find whatever it is I was missing.

I was still uncertain about so many things, I knew one thing I knew for sure: having a kid – planned or unplanned – without a relationship, simply to beat a ticking biological clock, was not the answer.

MASTERMINDING IN MOROCCO

O nce finished with the journaling assignment, four women, including myself, gathered in a small corner of a spacious garden courtyard at La Villa des Orangers Hotel and Spa in Morocco. The five-star resort was the idyllic setting for personal reflection that would allow us, all women entrepreneurs, to level up in our respective businesses. There was me, a writing and book editing coach, Deidre, a personal finance planner from Charlotte, North Carolina, and Ericka, a holistic career coach from Brooklyn, New York. We had all traveled thousands of miles to participate in a four-day business mastermind retreat created by Rosetta Thurman, a successful entrepreneurial coach for Black women.

On a patio overlooking a serene turquoise pool, we sat in a shaded sitting area, each of us nestled in comfy, low, rattan chairs with our feet resting on cushioned ottomans. Perfectly polished ivory stone pillars with intricate mosaic patterns anchored our space, along with a carved wooden table holding a silver kettle of mint tea and pastries. The sound of water trickling out of the sculptured fountain nearby, calmed our minds. The setting was the perfect combination of bohemian opulence and traditional Moroccan luxury.

For the past three days in the hotel's private meeting space, Rosetta had been guiding us through a series of business development assignments, designed to help us authentically market our services.

"Marketing and sales are two distinct elements. Powerful copywriting marries them together," said Rosetta. "Being real, getting personal about why you do what you do and how you use your gifts – they're essential for genuinely connecting with those you wish to serve. Now, let's hear what you wrote."

As someone who helped aspiring authors, I thought I had been pretty clear about my services on the website I developed during my time in Mexico. But, my site was more professional than personal. The assignment we had just finished wanted us to dig deeper. I wasn't used to talking about myself, my struggles, or my fears to anyone but my therapist; even she didn't always know everything.

But, in Morocco, for the first time, after adventures that included riding camels in the desert and haggling with vendors in the Souk, I was open to trying more new things.

"Nichole, you go first," said Rosetta. She sat comfortably cross-legged in her chair with an afro and a flowing linen ensemble, exuding the all-knowing guru vibe quite masterfully.

"Why is it important for you to help other women write their books?"

I opened my journal and read what I just wrote.

"Books provide an opportunity to experience another person's life. To share information and exchange ideas. They help others to learn and grow."

"It's just ok. A bit generic," said Deidre.

Really Deidre? I thought. Oh I couldn't wait until it was my turn to critique.

"I'm not feeling it. It sounds like a book report," commented Ericka.

As the writer of the group, I was surprised-not to mention a bit disappointed.

I thought it was a strong revision of my existing website text.

Rosetta began to give feedback. We all had grown accustomed to her signature warm-yet-tough love, in-your-face, do-better coaching over the past few days. Crazy enough, we actually welcomed it.

"They're right. Nichole, why are books so important to you? Why does it matter for more women to write books?"

I paused to think of a better answer. "Stories matter. Different voices matter. Writing shouldn't be an obstacle."

"And?"

I was getting frustrated. I wasn't used to not having the right answer. I could usually fake it pretty well. But Rosetta wasn't buying it.

In that moment, I gave up and just thought of the first thing that came to mind.

"Ok, I was a shy and quiet kid growing up. I didn't talk much and didn't want to. Instead, I just watched and observed. My mother told me that even when I was a toddler and learning how to talk, I didn't even babble much. I was so quiet that she'd have to look in the back seat when she was driving to make sure I was still there. As I grew older, I started finding my voice through writing. Everyone said I was good at it. Being understood through my words gave me confidence and courage. I want to help others discover and develop that same power."

I didn't know if it was the answer Rosetta was looking for. But, a dimmed, familiar passion flickered within me for the first time in a long while. Inspired and moved, the other participants nodded in approval.

"There's your pitch for your business and the beginning of your next book," said Rosetta with an approving look. "Start from there."

When I returned to Chicago, I knew I had finally reconnected to my purpose and passion for my first love: writing. For so many years growing up and even in college, writing had been my outlet, helping me to make sense of myself and the world. But over the past several years, while helping others to refine their voice, I'd forgotten about my own. Sure, I'd write about the happenings during my travels, but not about my day-to-day feelings. When I slowed down, so did my writing, which had been the friend I'd turned to whenever I was confused, lonely, and depressed. By writing from the heart, I found something missing that I didn't realize had disappeared.

The final draft of my new marketing copy went like this:

My mother tells me that when I was little, around three or four years old, I was really quiet. Although I knew how to speak, I just didn't. During car rides, she would keep looking back and check to make sure I was still there. I was that quiet.
I still don't speak much unless I have something to say. I'm not a fan of small talk.
But, if there's something important to say, I'll make sure I'm heard.
In these times, choosing to be silent, choosing to wait until everything is perfect is sometimes close to never.
I believe that now more than ever, we need to speak up.
Share our stories.
Share our truths.
Tell the world who we are and who we are not.

Make sure our voices and our stories are heard far and wide.

Because you better believe, there are others with opposing truths that are not hesitating or waiting.

I get it. It's risky to talk, to share about your life.

Especially your mistakes and lessons learned the hard way.

But, it's riskier if you don't.

People are dying and trying to figure out how to survive in trying times.

The knowledge you have can help them to not only survive but also to thrive.

Start speaking. Start writing and keep sharing.

Even if you have more questions than answers.

TRAVELING WHILE BLACK: WERE KANYE AND JAY-Z THE ONLY ONES IN PARIS?

Before owning a passport, I got used to navigating foreign spaces. Attending a private, predominantly White middle school, I got used to being the only Black girl in most of my classes. Even when I tried, I didn't fit in. I was frequently underestimated or overlooked by my classmates and sometimes my teachers, too. But it wasn't a big deal. I got used to not fitting in because my good grades proved that I belonged.

I got used to being the only one.

Eventually, I went to an all-Black public school. They said I was "too white" and that I talked funny. Once again, I didn't fit in.

So, I just got used to being alone and comfortable with being different.

Or so I thought.

I went to a majority White college, but there were quite a bit more Black people from all different backgrounds. We created our own community because we didn't fit in with the majority, only with each other. We gave each other a nod of recognition as we passed each other on campus. We sat together in the cafeteria. We found each other in large lecture halls. We formed student groups and looked out for each other. Being different was okay. Being smart was accepted.

Yet, out of four thousand Black students, I was surprised that during my senior year I was the only one enrolled in the Department of Music's study abroad program going to Africa. The other students joining me in South Africa were White. For the Blackest of the Black college experience – going to Africa – I would be the only Black person. When the ten of us met each other in Johannesburg to begin the six-week semester, I tried to hide my disappointment. Nevertheless, we all were excited to travel to Africa, most of us were out of the country for the first time in our lives.

I kind of already knew, but I really knew as the weeks went on, that despite having the exact same itinerary, my perspectives and experiences would be vastly different from my classmates. Unlike my peers, I was eager to go to Africa to learn about the social justice struggles that mirrored those of Black Americans. They were more interested in eating zebra meat and roughing it out in the wild, even though South Africa is a very Westernized nation. For them, their time in Africa was an exotic, adventurous escape from the everyday realities of home. For me, the contrast between the haves and have-nots, largely based on skin color, were instead extreme reminders of racial inequities at home that I had been studying for the past four years as a political science major.

My White classmates couldn't relate, and I wasn't about to explain what it was like to be a Black minority in a Black majority society and still experience oppression. Nor could they recognize the subtle, sometimes overt, racism I observed as we traveled throughout the post-apartheid country. Only six years after the end of apartheid, South Africa's struggle for racial equality was fresh in the memories of those who carried on with their day-to-day lives. The separation of Whites and anyone of color, although no longer mandated by law, was still visible. The stench of racism and discrimination crossed borders and international waters.

I didn't even have anyone I could talk to or relate to what I was going through. I had so many questions and feelings I could barely articulate. Why did the young South African kid at the orphanage ask me if I knew the rapper Puffy? Why was a spacey White lady hailed as the "expert" talking about the Zulu people as if it was an ancient, dead culture? Why did the waiter at the upscale Cape Town restaurant take everyone's order, but mine? How could our Indian tour guide drive by a Black African just hit by a car with blood coming from his head and point it out as if it were a tourist attraction? My feelings oscillated between admiration at the natural beauty of the continent and rage at the social injustices and ignorance of my fellow classmates. In Africa, I fit in, but because of being centuries removed from my homeland, I didn't belong.

Fifteen years later, the feeling was still the same. The more I traveled internationally as a flight attendant and the more places I went, the more I couldn't escape the smog of economic inequalities frequently based on race and ethnicity. Having a sociology education gave me a unique perspective different from my crew members, many of them who also had diverse cultural backgrounds. I noticed foreign tourists, mostly white, dominated mostly brown, once-colonized countries. It was disturbing to see local customs and culture treated as commodities – a source of entertainment and fascination. Although I was a tourist as well,

I always noticed with familiarity the haves and have-nots. Just like I noticed the curious stares from white tourists and locals alike. When I was off-duty and out of uniform, their expressions seemed to ask what I was doing there. Ignoring their stares, I was usually wondering, where are the other international travelers that look like me?

Despite the stares, I enjoyed getting out of the country. Mexico was my haven when off-duty. When working, most of my trips were to Europe. The short layovers gave me temporary reprieve from racial neuroses and the nonstop "buy this, buy that" consumer mindset of American culture. News channels were informative rather than dominated by excited chitchat about Trump's latest antics. In places like Britain, Spain, and France, although cut from the same colonization cloth, there seemed to be an air of sensibility, a collective maturity toward political and social matters. When visiting Europe, where racism exists in a different flavor although Black, I could also be simply an American and thus enjoying class status as a foreign tourist. Furthermore, my elite status as an airline crew member gave me access to upscale hotels where I was among the few, if not the only "one."

But, while I shopped, ate, and explored doing all the things that tourists do, I always saw the brown-and-black-skinned immigrants with distinctly African features that looked like mine. They were usually struggling and hustling while catering to those of lighter complexions who leisurely lounged and freely consumed. It reminded me that racial oppression is not an American invention. This awareness of a painful reality accumulated in my memory like carbon absorbs into the lungs. Like smoke, if you inhale too much at one time, eventually you'll begin to choke.

That's what racism was like for me, a heavy energetic or spiritual smog making it difficult to breathe and just be. For me, traveling was like pure oxygen – a break from the feeling of having the weight of the world on my shoulders. Exploring allowed me the escape I needed. My usual destinations were no longer sufficient. I needed to get further away from the nonsense and see something new. Plus, I was overdue for a trip anyway.

FINDING MY TRIBE IN THAILAND

Thailand was definitely farther away. It was on my bucket list of places to someday visit. All my coworkers and traveler friends had already been there. I envied their stories about getting up-close and personal with elephants and paying only six dollars an hour for foot massages. There wasn't anything stopping me from going to Thailand other than I didn't have a travel clique and I wasn't thrilled about going someplace so far and foreign by myself. Mexico was one thing, but traveling to Asia by myself was a level that I wasn't ready for. Sure, I could find an overpriced tour group to join, but even before being a flight attendant, I always opted for smaller, simpler, and less expensive trips.

When Marsha and Miguel announced that they would be going to Thailand instead of Mexico for their annual winter escape, I promised I would "stop by" to see them while they were in Chiang Mai. I couldn't pass up exploring a new place that I'd always wanted to visit with two of my favorite people. But, I knew I would only have five days to get there and back before I had to work another trip. It wasn't enough time to travel so far, but the elephants and spas were calling me.

Before I left, I also tracked down Anna, who was frequently traveling across the globe. She mentioned she and her boyfriend had been back and forth to Thailand on business. I looked forward to an opportunity to catch up with her while I was there. It had been years since I had seen Anna, but now and then, we kept in touch by text. She gave me a few Facebook groups for things to check out before and after I arrived in Thailand, in case she was gone before I arrived. One of the groups was Brothers and Sisters of Chiang Mai.

Three connecting flights and twenty-four hours later, I landed at the Chiang Mai International Airport in the late afternoon. Waiting for passengers outside of the airport exit were lines of bright red tuk-tuks that I had seen before in movies. Small Asian men whizzed by on these vehicles that were a cross between a bicycle, motorcycle, and a three-wheeled horse carriage, but without the horse. I approached a tuk-tuk and showed the driver the address of my hotel destination. He loaded my luggage and we zipped off into a sea of traffic. With dusty, curving roads and few traffic lights, it reminded me of Mexico. Open-air markets with vendors selling souvenirs, fruits, vegetables, cellphone accessories, and clothes lined both sides of the street. There were crowds of locals and tourists milling about everywhere.

I got a room at the same hotel as Marsha and Miguel. After getting settled in, I stopped by their room before they left to go to dinner. Halfway delirious from jet lag, we made plans to meet up the next day. Having arrived in Thailand a few weeks before me, they knew it would take an entire day for me to recover from my long travels. In three days, I had a long list of things I wanted to do, which included spending time with Marsha, Miguel, and Anna, in addition to finding an elephant sanctuary and trying different spas. Getting a manicure and pedicure on the cheap with all the glitter and designs I wouldn't dare pay for in Chicago was also on my to-do list.

I went to bed at 6:30 p.m. and woke up at 5 a.m., feeling as if it was the middle of the afternoon. Back in Chicago, it probably was. I was unsure of what to do at such an odd hour. It was still dark outside and I was never up at such a time unless I had to go to work. I sat down at the writing desk to journal and watch the sun come up from my hotel room window, which overlooked a placid winding river. It was a quiet, dramatic, amber globe, taking its time, bursting through the clouds.

Once again, I was engulfed in this surreal space of incredulity that this life of travel was mine. Although I traveled throughout Europe and the Americas, getting home always took less than a day. The language and customs, even though not my own, were familiar. Here in Asia, nothing was familiar. But, I wasn't lonely or fearful. A few floors below and even across town were friends who I could count on. Still tired, but happy and excited, I fell back asleep.

By the time I woke up again, it was late in the afternoon. Marsha and Miguel were out and about, with plans to return in the evening. In the meantime, I made plans to meet up with several people from Nomadness Travel Tribe who were in town for some type of filming event. Anna had mentioned that there were auditions for a Spike Lee film, which was puzzling to hear. Spike Lee in Thailand? I didn't know Chiang Mai was a destination for celebrities.

With directions from Google Maps, I took another tuk-tuk to a small restaurant and met up with three other members of the Nomadness Travel Tribe. They had all just met each other a day before. There was Travis, a travel writer with a slim build and smooth onyx skin. He appeared to be in his early twenties and could easily be mistaken for a student. Travis was on an assignment in Indonesia when he heard about an opportunity to be in a Spike Lee film. He changed his travel plans and delayed his return to London for a few days. The other young woman was Sophia, a Haitian-American with dreads that were pulled into a ponytail. Sophia had been living in Bangkok for several years and worked remotely as an IT specialist. The third person was Shevette, from North Carolina. She had flawless copper skin and short, cropped hair, dyed blond. She shared with us that she'd been traveling on a pilgrimage of sorts as she figured out what she wanted to do in the next chapter of her life.

They were still buzzing from excitement at the reception hosted by Spike Lee the night before I arrived and were amazed at how many Black people from all across the world had gathered for the monumental event. I felt as if I had been there. We marveled at how our life journeys had brought us to Thailand for the first time. After our meal of curries, spicy noodles, and seafood soups, the three of us wandered around the quirky, hipster Ninman area, taking pictures of one another in front of street art before going to a rooftop bar to watch the sunset.

Out of all my travels, this was the first time I'd met up with a group of Black travelers who were not docking from a cruise ship or venturing off from a resort. Traveling to Mexico, I'd always met Canadian, American, and European expats – all of whom were white. In Europe, I often met African immigrants, but never Americans. Sophia was the first Black American expat whom I had met.

"What's it like living in Bangkok?" I asked.

"I love it, I'm getting better at speaking Thai, which makes a huge difference."

"Everyone doesn't stare at you?"

"They are so used to seeing Black people around here.

Everyone's friendly, especially as long as you respect the customs."

Without any set itinerary, the three of us decided to meet up the next day and hang out. When researching things to do, Travis had heard about a waterfall that you could climb. It sounded improbable, but at one point in time, so too did traveling on my own to Asia.

Later that evening, I met up with Marsha and Miguel for dinner. We walked over to the Le Dta'wan Street Food Market. It was a night bazaar of every food imagined, from grilled seafood to barbecue steaks. The three of us wandered the stalls, trying to figure out what we wanted to eat. It was a festive atmosphere of roped lights strung above the food stalls as a live band played from a center stage. Miguel settled on a grilled vegetarian entrée, Marsha ordered a seafood platter, and I ordered a steak and stir-fry. We all shared one another's meals and enjoyed the warm night breeze.

After dinner, I went off on my own to meet up with Anna. She sent me a text to meet her at an open mic poetry event at a place called the Healing House. It was the same event that Travis, Sophia, and Shevette had mentioned earlier and were planning to attend.

The tuk-tuk dropped me off on a dark narrow side street and pointed to a dark house that looked unoccupied. I showed him the address that Anna sent me and he nodded again. I didn't think I was in the right location as I slowly got out of the tuk-tuk. Before I could turn around to ask him a second time, the driver had taken off. On a dark street in Chiang Mai, I was a bit nervous. I wandered down the street with a feeling that I was close as I could hear applause coming from somewhere nearby.

After a few minutes, a side door opened from an alley and Anna stepped out. We hugged and I quietly followed her inside. In an instant, I was transported back to an open mic night room that could have been any place in Chicago. Underneath red lights, a mixed crowd of twenty-and thirty-something Blacks, whites, and Asians sat on the floor and on the stairs of a living room, enjoying music and poetry. Heads nodded as the event host, a charcoal-skinned Black man sat casually on a makeshift stage, beatboxing into the microphone with the skills of a long time hip-hop artist.

Later in the evening, I learned that the host, Lawrence "Binkey" Tolfree, was a Southside Chicago native who found his refuge in Chiang Mai.

"Here, I don't have to worry about getting shot by the police," said Lawrence proudly. Binkey wasn't the only African-American living in Thailand who I met that night. Terrance, a basketball player from Nashville, expressed similar feelings. Playing for a Thai basketball team, Terrance and his girlfriend, Theresa, a hairdresser from Florida, had found their corner of paradise. They were not afraid of the local police, who befriended rather than harassed them.

Not long after I arrived and during the intermission, I left the mellow vibe of the Healing House with Anna, Terrance, and Theresa. They toured me through the crowded club districts of Chiang Mai, which consisted of a long street of open-air dance parties. There was a separate club for every genre of music, from country to pop to hip-hop. Each space competed for who could play their music the loudest and attract the largest gathering for mostly foreign young revelers. As we weaved our way through the different clubs and through the dancing crowds, we stopped and chatted with other expats that Anna, Theresa, and Terrence knew. It seemed like everyone knew everyone, and most of them were Black, which surprised me the most. All of them were simply out, enjoying another weekend night of drinking and partying.

As the parties thinned out promptly at midnight, the four of us strolled through the city that grew quieter as we moved farther away from the party district. We went to the late-night fruit stand to grab a smoothie. Anna and I chatted as if we'd seen each other last week. Years later, she was still strikingly beautiful with the outgoing personality. She looked exactly the same too, as if she had not aged a bit.

Over the next few days in Chiang Mai, I met so many more Black expats from Africa, the Caribbean, Europe, as well as the United States. There was the Ghanaian military veteran who had lived in Thailand for over twenty years. The young student from London who was running an online business. A New York real estate investor and several writers. These were just a few of the more than more than forty Blacks of all ages that attended a weekly Sunday dinner. Some were expats who had lived in Chiang Mai for decades, others were visiting for a few months.

Over and over, they shared with me how much they enjoyed Thailand. I could feel their sense of happiness and community. By living in Thailand, they had found a way to hack the oppressive nature of racism by leaving the United States and other parts of the world to create their own path to liberation. It was a community of expats who found the freedom to not just travel but also to exist beyond the conventions of their upbringings in order to have a better quality of life. Some taught English as a second language, some were studying abroad, and others were online business owners or artists.

From Mexico to Chicago, around the world and back, I had never found my tribe until I went to Thailand. Elsewhere, I had discovered either tourists or residents, but never Black expats. As a part of several travel groups, I'd become familiar with more Black people who frequently traveled overseas as a way of life. However, I had never met so many Black Americans living overseas who didn't have a corporate job of some type. I rarely met others around my age who were single and shared my passion for new experiences outside the norm. Finally, I'd connected with a conscious group of true global citizens who were aware of their privilege to travel, live, and create a sense of community anywhere in the world.

While in Thailand, I didn't see Marsha and Miguel as much as I planned. Had I not lost an entire day trying to get my phone that I had dropped in a waterfall repaired, I would have caught up with them earlier. Now, the final night before they were leaving for Bangkok for the next part of their travels, I saw them again at the hotel. I was staying behind in Chiang Mai since I only had two more days in Thailand.

"We waited around for you in Chiang Mai and we hardly saw you," said Miguel, half-teasing.

"I know, I'm sorry." I said, feeling guilty. "I was so busy partying and climbing waterfalls with my new friends."

In the past few days I had had more of a social life in Chiang Mai than I did over the past few months in Chicago. There was so much to do and see, much of which Marsha and Miguel had already experienced before my arrival.

"Ignore him," said Marsha. "I'm glad you're having fun. We'll see you back in Chicago."

After Marsha and Miguel left for Bangkok, I spent the next two days exploring by myself. I had enjoyed meeting so many new people, but I needed some time to myself. Alone, I could settle into my familiar cautiously curious mood as I wandered around during the day to the different temples in Old City taking pictures of ornate Buddha statues and elaborate decor. Whenever I got tired of walking, I ducked into the closest spa for a foot massage. At night, I visited crowded markets, carefully selecting souvenirs that included hand-carved flower soaps, candles, and incense.

For my final day, I booked a half-day tour at an elephant sanctuary right outside the city. I joined a group of about fifteen tourists, many of them young backpackers, for an hour-long bus ride to the rural area South of Chiang Mai. Upon arrival, we were awestruck by the size of the elephants. As promised, we got up close and personal with the elephants, all of us taking turns petting and feeding them. The friendly creatures eagerly grabbed bunches of bananas from our hands with their trunks and stuffed them into their mouths. After their morning breakfast, we followed the herd down to the river and helped the caretakers give the elephants mud baths. Many of us doted over the baby elephant that delightfully rolled around in the water as we coated it with mud. Laughing, all of us jumped out of its way to avoid getting splashed or stepped on. The day ended and we said our goodbyes to the caretakers, our guides, and the elephants. It was another unforgettable once-in-a-lifetime experience.

During the ride back to the city, where I would pack up for the long trek back home, I felt as if my time in Thailand was a beginning rather than an end. I wasn't sure when, but I would be back.

I returned to Chicago, excited about the possibilities again. I stayed in touch by Facebook with many of the Black expats who I had met during my short visit. Popping up frequently in my feed now were pictures of Black travelers in Thailand, who I now knew personally. Their serene smiling faces meditating in nature and writing about their holistic living practices inspired me. It brought me joy to see thriving Black men and women successfully creating an unconventional life on their own terms outside of America. My trip to Thailand reignited a desire to be connected to myself, to others, and to the world.

It also made me ask myself: what did liberation look like for me?

I hadn't figured it out just yet, but I was getting there. It had something to do with travel, with words, and finding a place of my own where I would always feel at home. I'd have to spend more time there, but perhaps Thailand would be that home, that community, and a place where I could truly be free.

I was uncertain, but in the meantime, another amazing travel experience was imprinted in my memory and on my iPhone camera roll.

SHHHH

A faint knock on the thin wooden door of the tiny bedroom quarters startled me awake.

"Nichole?" said Helene from the other side. Her voice was soft yet concerned. "Are you okay?"

The small digital clock on the nightstand read 6:10 a.m.

Shit!

Five more minutes had turned into twenty. I slept straight through the warning gong and was missing the required morning meditation session.

Like a problem pupil, I was now being personally escorted by the teacher's assistant.

"Coming," I said as I jumped out of bed to open the door. Her friendly eyes greeted me with a forgiving smile.

Embarrassed, I muttered an apology and grabbed my coat. I felt like a twelve-year-old who hadn't learned to wake up and get to class on time.

Helene waited patiently by the door as I tied my gym shoes. I had originally woken up and gotten dressed at 5 a.m. After going to breakfast, I returned to the dormitory to get a few more minutes of sleep before the start of our 6 a.m. meditation session.

It was only day two of a ten-day silent meditation retreat. If sitting cross-legged for twelve hours a day would be one challenge, I guess waking up at the butt crack of dawn for eight more days would be the other.

Several months after returning from Thailand, I decided to give meditation another shot. I was inspired by the tranquil temple gardens throughout Chiang Mai and the quiet discipline of the Buddhist monks I met. Now that I had new Facebook friends from Thailand, images of Black men and women from all walks of life touting the benefits of meditation as a path to inner peace flooded my news feed. It was encouraging to see that meditation for the first time was not simply an appropriated New Age thing for hippies and skinny yoga girls.

In the past, meditation was never my thing. High-performing entrepreneurs and celebrities touted the ancient practice as their secret to success and greater self-awareness. When we were together, Max often told me about his experiences and encouraged me to keep trying. I knew it would be good for me to do, but like yoga, I couldn't get into it. I tried different types of meditation, solo and in groups, but sitting still, closing my eyes, and breathing usually ended up with me falling asleep. Other times, five minutes would feel like five hours in the noisy shopping mall of my mind.

Despite many failed attempts to develop some kind of practice, I was determined to keep at it. As with learning a new language, maybe an immersion experience of a multiday class or retreat would help. Plus, it would be another good excuse to travel (as if I ever really needed an excuse).

After asking friends and doing a bit of research, I learned about Vipassana meditation retreats. Although there were centers all over the world, the only available upcoming dates were in Pecatonica, Illinois, a rural area located an hour-and-a-half outside of Chicago. *Well*, I thought, *I wouldn't be too distracted with exploring a new, exotic place.* A ten-day retreat was a bit longer than I preferred and seemed far from a luxury experience, but the course, which included meals and lodging, was free. According to the website, students would "Learn the basics of the method and practice sufficiently to experience its beneficial results."

I found "the catch" in the website – The Code of Discipline (even the term sounded a bit cultish): no phones, no computers, or other electronic gadgets were allowed. No reading, writing, exercising, or listening to music was allowed during a participant's stay. Oh, and no talking or interacting with any other participants. The focus was strictly on meditation for ten days straight.

So, it would be just me, alone with my thoughts, day in and day out for ten days?

Whoa.

The crisp autumn air seeped through my unzipped winter coat as Helene and I briskly walked in silence to the meditation hall. It was a short walk from the women's dorm to the neighboring building along a narrow gravel pathway. I listened to the stones that were crunching beneath our feet with each step. It was still pretty dark, but the sun was starting to come up from over the adjacent cornfields. By the time we arrived at our destination, I was fully awake from the cold. Going away for meditation training had sounded like a such good idea in theory, but in practice, not so much.

The entry corridor of the meditation hall was only slightly warmer than outside. The place wasn't a hall or a temple, but rather a one-story ranch farmhouse with a large pond on a small acre of land with trees and open fields. I took off my shoes and hung my coat in the mudroom. Helene opened the door, directing me into the quiet, dimly lit meditation space. I was not in trouble and didn't have to speak to anyone – I was just late.

Crowded into the space, a large, carpeted room, were rows of other participants who were silently sitting on the floor along with a few neatly arranged chairs along the walls of the room. I stepped as quietly as possible through the rows of students until I found my assigned space from the previous day. The mountain of pillows to support my back, butt, and legs were arranged just as I had left them last night. The room was so quiet, you could hear the creaking of the door as it closed behind me. Every cough, sniffle, and heavy breath broke the eerie silence of our meditation sessions. On more than one occasion, I could hear faint snoring that, thankfully, wasn't coming from me.

The two teachers from yesterday, one man and one woman, were sitting in lotus position at the front of the room. It looked as if they had been sitting for hours rather than just fifteen minutes. From their elevated platform, they exuded a sense of calm. The dark room was cozy and almost perfect for going back to sleep. If I could only figure out how to sit comfortably upright when I really wanted to lie down and nap like a preschooler. But, as instructed the previous evening, I sat with legs crossed in an uncomfortable lotus position on the pillows, wrapped myself in a blanket, and closed my eyes. I did my best to keep my mind focused on my breath along the itty-bitty space between my upper lip and nostrils, as instructed.

Should our minds wander, we were directed to gently bring it back from wherever it went and focus on breathing. Easier said than done. Of course, my mind didn't simply wander – it constantly and recklessly raced around in circles, just like the screaming little Speedy Gonzales mouse in the cartoons.

Only five hours until lunch. What would they serve? I hoped it was as tasty as yesterday. Aw man, I forgot to brush my teeth. I really need to work on my flexibility. Damn, I'm still cold. I should have grabbed another blanket. Seriously, my foot is already falling asleep. I wish I was still asleep. Maybe I should stretch in the mornings. Probably at night, too. Did I turn the heat off in the apartment? The lights? Lights flashing. I never thought that I would make it faaaaaaar. Thailand was far. Elephants! I miss Mexico. Tacos. You don't have to call, it's ookaaaaay girl, cuz I'mma be alright toooo-niiiiight. Breath one, breath two...ugh. Oh yeah, I'm supposed to be breathing. How many muscles are in the nose? Why do we only have two nostrils and not three? What time is it? I'm ready for lunch. I'm guessing there's twenty minutes left until lunch. Focus. Focus. Focus! Dammit!

Silence.

Okay, just breathe.

Spaghetti maybe?

By the third day, I was starting to get the hang of things. Starting at four thirty in the morning until nine at night, we were on a regimented schedule that consisted of meditation, a meal, or a short break. It was rigorous, but not quite torturous. We had little free time and very little to do except our personal grooming. There was nothing to do either. During lunch breaks, I walked around the tractor-cut area in a grassy field behind the women's dorm. Walking was the only permitted exercise.

Although I couldn't help but be aware of the other thirty or so people around, we were instructed not to interact or communicate with one another. Occasionally and unconsciously, you briefly locked eyes. While eating at the dining hall, you ate in silence while looking around at your surroundings, which included everyone else doing the same thing as you. Throughout the course, and only if needed, you quietly communicated with hand gestures solely for logistical purposes such as who arrived first to stand in lines to the bathroom or cafeteria buffet.

I was surprisingly not as lonely as I imagined I would be. Although we weren't talking, we weren't alone unless when we were in our single-bed dorm room. Everyone was absorbed in their own inner world. I could tell I wasn't the only one who was struggling with the schedule that consisted of waking up ridiculously early and sitting for insanely long hours.

By day four, the newness was wearing off and the days were starting to drag along. Wake up. Eat. Meditate. Meditate more. Eat. Meditate. Meditate. Evening tea break. Meditate. Meditation instructions for tomorrow. Rest and repeat.

Despite my growing mound of pillows for my back, knees, and legs, everything still ached most of the time. My flexibility sucked. I constantly shifted from one position to another, and when it got too bad, I hugged my knees. With students alongside me, there wasn't much room for stretching my legs out in front of me. I tried not to make a lot of noise when I shifted my body. Despite all this, my mind was slowing down. Thoughts weren't recklessly running anymore; it was more of a slow, steady, jog that kept me mildly amused.

On the fifth day, our practice changed up a bit.

"Today, we are going to refrain from major movements of your body," said the teacher. "Keep your hands and arms in the same position. If you feel a nose itch, just let it itch."

Wait, I had just figured out what subtle movements would give me a reasonable amount of relief when needed, and now I'm not supposed to move at all?

Forget this cross-legged thing, I needed a chair. Helene accommodated me with a tiny folding chair. Unable to stretch my legs because there were others sitting on the floor in front of me, I might as well have been sitting in a middle seat of an airplane or in the exit row, which doesn't recline. Sitting in the chair with my knees bent at exactly ninety degrees didn't help, it was actually worse. I went back to sitting on the floor. During our short breaks, I looked around to see misery and discomfort in everyone's eyes as we stretched our limbs and left to use the bathroom.

The only respite of the evenings was a thirty-minute video lesson featuring a jovial, older Indian man with a baritone voice and heavy accent. In the dated video recording, he would explain to us the importance of the meditation techniques we were learning.

After six days of silence, I started talking in my sleep. In the middle of the night, I woke myself up (and probably everyone else in the women's dorm) yelling, "Thank you!" to an imaginary person in my dreams.

Startled awake and slightly embarrassed, I listened for a minute to disturbed bodies shifting in beds before I fell back to sleep. If you could hear every creak, cough, and sigh through the thin walls separating the fifteen of us from one another, you could definitely hear if someone was talking.

The next morning, on day seven, I slept in and went to breakfast late. For the past two days, it had been cloudy and cold. I hadn't been sleeping well, and although clean, the room was dusty and the air was dry. I occasionally fell asleep during meditation.

If I couldn't even manage to be quiet in my sleep, how in the world could I silence my mind to master this meditation thing? This was not going how I imagined. I really wanted to get this meditation thing right. I'm not sure why, but I just knew that calming my mind through meditation would unlock some new door of hidden potential within me. Perhaps, it would be a pathway to happiness. Plus, I was just used to being a good student and getting things right.

Even the course participants were starting to get on my nerves, even though I had not met or spoken to anyone. Especially the tall girl with the ridiculously long hair down to her waist who sat in front of me during meditation. Her worst offense was not her hair, but one morning, she took the pink slippers I'd been wearing for the past six days. Sure, they weren't mine, but every morning, every afternoon, and evening during mealtime, I changed from my shoes into the slippers at the entrance of the dining. They were the only ones in the row of slippers at the entrance of the dining hall that fit my large, flat feet. But, for some reason on day six, she arrived to the hall before me and changed up her slipper selection. Because of her, I had to miserably eat lunch in my socks with cold feet.

More misery. More suffering.

Three long days left.

I was ready to go home back to my studio apartment. I wanted to get a chicken, maybe steak, or a burrito from my favorite Mexican takeout spot. Did all the meals have to be vegetarian? My butt was sore from sitting. I needed more cushions. I needed a chair. I really needed a burrito. What day is it? What if my apartment burns down while I'm gone? Maybe Trump will be impeached by the time I get back...

I walked back to my dorm for the break, thinking about the slipper injustice. I stewed about not having them on while I ate my breakfast.

But, did you die?

The voice from inside my head reminded me that I was being so petty. It wasn't that deep, but with nothing else to focus on, my mind needed something to complain about. I laughed at my own absurdity. Yup, I was officially going loony.

In that moment, I realized I was making myself miserable. I was engrossed in my complaints and creating more misery than necessary. I caught myself as I spiraled down to an unwarranted state of sadness. Fed up with my internal whining, I just let my irritation go. I was breathing, well-fed, and all my bills were paid.

I am fine, I thought as I felt the wind tickle the space above my nostrils and looked over at the brilliant colors of the sun that were rising over in the fields.

I was awestruck by the stillness and beauty of the morning.

On day eight, the sadness and fatigue lingered. I nestled into discomfort and accepted it without complaining that my knees would hurt and my legs would get stiff. My back would eventually ache. I just needed to focus on the instructions given and double down my efforts to focus.

Sometime during day nine, the hour-long sessions weren't long enough.

I was eager for the next.

During breaks, I would return early to the meditation hall, just to sit and practice before everyone else arrived. Surprisingly, my legs were a bit more flexible from all the days of sitting, so I reduced the mountain of pillows propping up my back, legs, and knees. They still hurt, just not as bad, allowing me to better concentrate on the meditation tasks.

We were told to simply sit still and take note of the sensations, but to not judge if they were pleasant or unpleasant. Our job was to just notice every little detail of whatever we were feeling, to observe our body as it relaxed and tensed. Give neutral and equal attention to the slightest itch, sharp pains, and dull aches. Allow them to emerge, recede, or simply persist without resistance.

As I surrendered, I sat and felt all the subtle and intense sensations moving throughout my body at the same time. There were strong and subtle ones happening at the same time vying for my attention. Aches and pains emerged and receded as I sat stoically. Sharp pains of muscles became dull aches. Intense itches that went unscratched eventually disappeared. I watched my mind's responses to these feelings come and go with indifference. My mind and my body were undergoing constant states of change. I was to neither embrace nor push away such change. Simply observe it for what it was; temporary and fleeting. In that moment, things were constantly transforming. Such change was triggered sometimes by internal or external occurrences. And sometimes, by nothing at all.

Over the past few years, I had traveled to so many places in the world. My surroundings frequently changed. So, too, did my circumstances. Some changes were more exciting than others. And, when it became too dull, I could pack up and get on a plane.

But, by sitting in the same place for days, I discovered that there was so much to explore within myself. Beyond my thoughts and feelings, there was this vast, dynamic universe with constantly colliding atoms, creating stimuli and responses from moment to moment. I was the owner and observer of all this! Sensations emerged and then subsided. They were mysterious, powerful, and comforting. The meditation techniques we learned were simply a map of how to get to a magical space within.

Immersed in practice without any day-to-day distractions, I successfully learned how to meditate. I could finally feel a positive difference as I sat, and after I opened my eyes at the conclusion of our mid-morning session.

If brainwashing was part of the Vipassana course and the teachings, our minds were definitely cleaner, more relaxed, and open for our last teaching at the end of day nine. The now-familiar Indian man on the video monitor who we all felt we now knew personally encouraged us to share our newfound peace with others by embodying generosity, compassion, and goodwill to every living being we encountered. There was no mention of a deity, a religious text to follow, or a follow-up class for only

$999. We were simply encouraged to continue our new practice and find ways to bring joy rather than harm to the world. That was something I could definitely support.

On day ten, noble silence officially ended without fanfare at 11 a.m., and talking was permitted once outside the meditation hall. When the teacher dismissed us, some students quietly trickled out of the meditation hall while others, including myself, sat for a while longer, knowing it would be the last time in what had become the perfect meditation space. Eventually, I ended my session and returned to the dorm room and was greeted with a burst of welcoming shouts as I opened the door to the building. All of the women students were sitting together in the hallway talking and laughing with one another. We chatted about the teachers, our hurting knees, and our assumptions about one another. We shared our biggest challenges and revelations as if we had been lifelong friends.

An hour later, as we packed up our things to depart, I was drained from talking and listening. Sound hitting our ears felt like light in our eyes after days of darkness. It was exciting, yet overwhelming, as we stretched communication skills that had grown stiff.

When I got to my car, which was parked in a lot on the edge of campus, I turned on my phone. I set it on silent as it started to ping and vibrate with notifications. I wasn't ready to respond to all the "Welcome back!" and "How's it going?" texts just yet. Instead, I drove back to Chicago in silence. There was an undercurrent of calm that wasn't there before, a buzz of energy still flowing within and around my body. I felt the sensations come and go. Over the next few days, I remained separate, but not estranged from my own thoughts, speech, and emotions, as well as those coming from other people around me.

Everything around me was so loud, unsteady, constantly changing, and beautiful.

EPILOGUE: FLIGHT ATTENDANTS ON THE COVID FRONTLINE

I landed back at O'Hare from vacationing in Guatemala with a renewed sense of gratitude for where my journey had led thus far. I'd just spent the past three weeks off-duty, reflecting and writing about the last eight years of my life working as a flight attendant. Life hadn't turned out anything like I had once planned, but it had so many of the things that I truly wanted – freedom, joy, and authentic relationships. Although I did not have the romantic kind of love yet, I had lasting love from family and friends. Still tripping and stumbling along the way, I was getting better at learning how to just be, no matter the circumstances. I was single, but never really alone.

Then unexpectedly, the world around me slowed down before coming to a sudden, screeching halt in mid-March of 2020. Two days back from traveling, it was like any other post-travel routine. I'd spent a few days in my apartment, keeping to myself and decompressing while unpacking and repacking before flying out again. The night before my first work trip after vacation, I sat down in front of my computer to catch up on company emails and read the news a bit closer. While I was away, I hadn't paid too much attention to what was going on in other parts of the world.

That night, scrolling Facebook and CNN, I perused reports of several school closings and a few reports of localized outbreaks of a virus from China that resembled the flu. In my inbox were friendly corporate reminder emails suggesting that flight attendants wash their hands more often in light of recent news events. Most of us did that already anyway, though. We knew planes were flying Petri dishes. Another email instructed us to keep an eye out for sick passengers traveling from China. This virus thing was of concern for many, but not too serious unless working to or from China, which was rare for me as a junior flight attendant. I was grateful, however, that I had heeded Anna's warning and hadn't gone all the way to Thailand to write this book. When I texted her, she mentioned that she and her boyfriend, who frequently visited Bangkok, were planning to return to the States.

Reporting to the airport on a Friday morning, O'Hare buzzed with passengers coming and going. I noticed foot traffic was a bit lighter than usual, but figured it was just slow before the start of spring break travel. My first flight of the day was surprisingly empty, with only twenty passengers heading to Baltimore. This usually meant that the subsequent return flight would be full.

From news reports, I expected passengers and crew to be slightly more on edge. Like me, my coworkers were concerned, but they didn't appear stressed out about it. They shared with me that most of the flights they worked had been unusually empty for the past week. During our pre-flight briefing, the captain re-emphasized that we keep an eye out for anyone appearing sick. As I greeted boarding passengers, I noticed only a handful wearing surgical masks or gloves. Several wiped down their seats and tray tables with sanitizing wipes they brought from home before sitting down. In-flight, the crew washed our hands with more frequency. I already wore gloves to pick up trash. The only policy change related to service was to use new glassware every time we poured a drink, instead of refilling the empty ones like we usually did. The return flight from Baltimore back to Chicago was also light, with only forty passengers.

Over the next two days of my trip, I constantly checked the news on my phone for updates between flights. More schools across the country were beginning to close. Travel to China was abruptly suspended.

I landed back in O'Hare with another two-day trip scheduled for the next day. Travel to Europe was suspended. All Chicago public schools were closed. This was getting serious. The last flight of my day was full with international passengers with connecting flights returning from overseas. In the small space, I tried to keep my distance as the flight attendant commuting home from Germany chatted with other crew members about the long lines in customs and the screening exemptions for crew, including herself.

My concern grew to alarm when New York went on lockdown. If this virus was spreading, all the hand washing in the world wouldn't prevent flight attendants from getting sick, as we were required to sit shoulder to shoulder on the jump seat with coworkers who were exempt from international screening so they could quickly get to their next flight. As I walked down the aisle pouring drinks and collecting trash, I cringed whenever I heard a passenger cough, sneeze, or sniffle.

I was uneasy with just one leg left to go for the day to Newark. I checked my schedule before we began the next boarding. I hadn't noticed until that moment that my layover hotel was an unfamiliar one in downtown New York and over an hour away from the airport. Whether it was a scheduling oversight or intentional, I was not going to stay in the outbreak epicenter for nineteen hours. If my request for a different hotel was denied by scheduling, I would stay in the airport crew room, sitting upright in a chair for the night. I sighed with relief when my request was granted to stay at a Newark hotel closer to the airport with no questions asked. Technically off-duty when I arrived for the night in Newark, I changed my final deadhead flight of my trip to an earlier one the next day and left early the next day to return to Chicago.

Relieved to get home, I monitored the Facebook groups for airline employees. Flight attendant posts from JetBlue United, Southwest, Delta, and American:

Not feeling well.

Sick.

Trying to get tested.

Exposed.

Quarantined in hotel.

Alone.

Notifications popped up on my phone as the scheduled flights for my next trip in a few days started to cancel. The one leg to Seattle, the other outbreak epicenter, had not. My family called to see where I was and if I was safe. They were fearful. I was fearful.

If I got sick or exposed during a trip, I could be quarantined away from home and alone.

I didn't want to go to work. But, could I afford to take off? If so, for how long?

As Chicago shut down, flight attendants were classified as essential workers. We were exempt from curfews. We could go to work and transport spring breakers returning from Florida.

I could go to work. But, for the first time ever, I didn't feel safe going.

The Seattle flight was finally canceled the night before departure. I'd already called off what was left of my trip. From home, I constantly checked the news and read new work emails as they came in. Changes and new in-flight service procedures were being implemented each day – the ones that should have been in place weeks if not months ago. Friendly reminders were now bleak, grim statements about unprecedented financial loss. It was like the weeks following 9/11 all over again, but it was terror of a different kind. We could take time off, unpaid, if needed. There were subtle hints of layoffs in the near future. There were more reports of sick flight attendants in our private Facebook groups along with photos of unsafe crowded flights transporting cruise ship passengers. Flight attendant death notices began showing up in the group feed.

When the seatbelt sign is on, half of our job is constantly informing passengers that it's not safe to move about the cabin. During takeoff, landing, and turbulence, we instruct them to remain seated even though flight attendants may still be up and about. We're trained to perform our duties with some turbulence. But, there are moments when the captain instructs everyone, including flight attendants, to return to their seats and fasten their seatbelts. We stop what we're doing, put away the carts, and quickly strap ourselves in. Call lights, refills, and snacks will have to wait.

Despite the illuminated sign and repeated announcements, there's always at least one passenger on every flight that gets up anyway. They open overhead bins, walk through the aisles, and go to the bathrooms. Sometimes, they even come to the galley just to stand and stretch their legs because they're tired of sitting. The obnoxious ones will attempt to negotiate with us and scoff in annoyance when we tell them to return to their seats. They have to go really bad. We don't stop them, but should they seriously injure themselves, we can make sure our incident report states that we informed them that the seatbelt sign is on.

It's not safe to be up and about, but, for whatever reason, these passengers are willing to take their chances.

I'm not willing to take my chances.

Turbulence can be dangerous if your seatbelt isn't fastened. Especially during storms, the plane shakes back and forth, like a sailboat on choppy waters. If I'm safely strapped in, I'm fine. I kind of like it – it's like a free rollercoaster ride. I'm confident I'm safe so I might as well enjoy the break. There's nothing I can do except sit and wait for the captain to tell us when it's over. Like passengers, flight attendants are eager to get up and get off the plane too. But, even after we land, as we taxi, we stay seated and strapped in until the plane is parked at the gate. We also have to wait until the seatbelt sign finally goes off.

I haven't been working for thirty days now. It will be a month, maybe more, before I return to work – I'm at home on leave. Remaining seated. Most of the time, I sit on my couch. I sit at my desk. I never imagined being a flight attendant and now I couldn't imagine a life not being a flight attendant.

But, as I lean into uncertainty and an unimagined future, I'm okay with sitting down and staying strapped in until the turbulence subsides.

I'll patiently wait for it to be safe to move about the cabin and the world.

ACKNOWLEDGMENTS

Although I'm a long-time writer, writing this book about all my personal business was so much harder than I thought it would be. There were days I truly enjoyed it and then there the many other days that I just had to keep writing although I wasn't feeling it. Overall, it was a cathartic process that not only takes time and focus, but a willingness to go back to relive the great and not-so-great memories.

As I write this, I shake my head at the goal to get my book done is six months, let alone three of those months were in 2020.

Just when I thought I told a good story, my skilled and wonderful editor ripped it to shreds, which is when the revision journey began. So first, a big thanks to Deidre Hammons of Lotus Prose, who edits as my writing partner elevated what began as a news report to a true book draft and finally into a manuscript that I can be proud of.

Ranka, my graphic designer for giving me the perfect book cover design even better than the one I had loosely envisioned. Thank you to my Fiverr beta reader Gabrielle whose developmental insights and suggestions stepped it up a notch further.

Thank you to my journalism colleagues Dawn and Megan for their awesome "can you take a look at this right quick?" edits, their encouragement on all of my writing and professional endeavors, and most importantly for their lifelong friendship. I finally got my book done and honored to know you'll be celebrating with me!

To all of the beta readers and friends especially Monica, and Josh for their early feedback. Whether you read a few chapters or just a paragraph, every bit of feedback made a huge difference to keep going on the days I didn't feel like writing. To Tiffany, girl, I think we've seen each other around the base maybe a total of two, maybe three times in eight years, but I truly value our friendship, your brilliant insights and just do it advice. I will never forget, even before my mom did, you were the first to pre-order my book! A special shout out to Rachael, every writer needs affirmation. Your honest enthusiasm and critique for this book meant so much. Thank you for such the awesome review. And to my Beta listeners too - all those who listened to me read a chapter or two aloud and didn't fall asleep. Instead, you helped me figure out what was clear and what was not. To the women of my business Mastermind groups that held me accountable to my deadlines. The members of the Story Skills workshop and BiPoc group especially who gave me a space to process and powerfully write about my experiences with race. Being a part of a community of deep thinkers and talented writers reminded me that I am not alone.

To my homegirl, bestie and partner in crime, Malaika, who knows the many stories I would not dare to even write down. I love you always chica. Here's to the many more travel memories we will create in this lifetime together. To my Sands and Sorors, I still mean it, wherever I am in the world, I'm here for you too! Thank you for all of your love and support. To Marci (reminder: passport), Professor's mom and all my friends who listen to me lament this past year about how long this was taking me to finish this damn book and all the hiccups along the way.

To all the men, I've dated or did something like that; the ex-boyfriends, lovers and the frogs. Thanks for the lessons and the memories. The laughter, adventure and the tears all had a purpose.

To my clients including late Alice Faye. I wish you here for my book launch. Thank you for believing in my talent and giving me the honor of serving as your editor. It's been a while since I've been the author's club and I think of you often.

My Chicago family: Marsha, my Chicago Mom and my Chicago Dad, as promised, I'm including your full name: Miguel Angelo Retana. I promise to always forward your fan mail with the longest letters from me. I love you both. And Mike, thanks for being who you wonderfully are and sharing your family. Eternal gratitude. My cousins, Travis, Dorthulia and Greg who are a part of why I love Chicago so much. Christina, Rachel, Tomiko, and Katie – I've always wanted friends who truly "get me" and I am so thankful to consider each of you a true friend. Terrell, writing about our adventures in and out of Chicago is a whole another book! Thanks for helping me figure out the last few chapter titles while working away from home in Dominican Republic. Shout out to my travel goals friend Irma – I know, our good times aren't mentioned here, but they are significant, nonetheless.

My family across the pond: Until our next reunion. I think the Chicago crew should now come to Brighton whenever the borders open again.

My Mexico family Joanne, Patricia, Lucilla, Gabby, Rose, Sarah, Lisa and Milan by way of Germany. Dulce, Juanita and Dylan. Stephanie and Cat – the experiences we shared, those included and excluded will also be a part of my heart and memories.

To my Guatemala crew Nigel, Santos, Kendra, Emily, Sonnie and Mara. During my days of writing the draft in lake Atitlan, your kind hearts and energy from our genuine friendship fueled my creative spirit and fed my spirit.

My co-workers at the airlines that shall not be named as well as my international flight attendant friends: Thank you for just being a part of the many memories in this book and many more. There are so many unforgettable memories of the camaraderie, adventure and laughter that are not in this book but noteworthy, nonetheless. It was so hard when I had to edit out some of the greatest memories. Our job isn't a job, it really is a way of life weather we're employed or not. Jet fuel really does get in our blood and flying, the desire to help even the worst of passengers becomes not just an obligation, but it's an addiction and even a passion. Weather for a short flight or friends for a lifetime, we'll always be family. Shout out to my favorite flight attendant Damon just for truly being the greatest.

Maria, Deb, My Landmark fam, Travis, Alton, Impact, all of my former clients and colleagues who were such an important part of my life story that led up to this flight attendant chapter.

My family family: My aunts, uncles, all of my crazy second cousins and my not-so-little-anymore first cousins that pre-ordered a book simply because they heard I was writing one. As I travel the world, miss birthdays, family reunions, weddings and funerals, please know that despite the distance, I'm always sending my love. Often, I think of how blessed I am to be a part of such a talented, amazing and loving family. You all will give me plenty of inspiration for the characters in my upcoming fiction books!

To Dad and Stepmom, thank you and I love you. Dad, your encouragement to pursue my writing has meant more than I tell you. I know that you are proud, and I am loved.

To my big brother, since you wrote a book first, I naturally I have to write a book that's better than yours. I love you. I look forward to you and sister-in-law sharing your journey in an upcoming book perhaps. To my favorite niece and nephew (you know who you are), I love you to pieces always. More travel adventures in Chicago and beyond await us.

To my Mama who asked me on every single phone call about the book – Yes, your baby has finally finished it – now you know a lot more of my personal business than I would probably ever tell you. Your strength, intelligence, resilience and faith always inspires me to do great things such as tell good stories. Thank you for your never-ending concern, love and encouragement. I am so honored to be your daughter. If I haven't told you today, I love you. And Stepdad, thank you for being a blessing in not just my mama's life, but mine too!

To God aka The Source, The Creator within me and surrounding me; the one who keeps me safe and protected always. Thank you for the many blessings and gifts you have bestowed upon me including this amazing life. I pray constantly that my actions and deeds, including this book are a true reflection of You.

ABOUT THE AUTHOR

Nichole L. Davis (not her real name) aka "Chi McFly" is a Chicago-based flight attendant for a global airline that shall also remain anonymous. A lifelong writer, avid reader and serial entrepreneur, Nichole has a passion for trying new things and living life to the fullest. When not traveling or catching up on sleep, you can find her working out, relaxing on a beach or spending time with her niece and nephew. She has a love for family and friends, books, red wine (Malbec), music, great photography and internet memes.

This is Nichole's first published book. However, you can find more of her writings on a defunct blog called Released to Crew Rest that she may someday revive.